CAMBRIDGE LIBRARY COLLECTION

Books of enduring scholarly value

English Men of Letters

In the 1870s, Macmillan publishers began to issue a series of books called 'English Men of Letters' – biographies of English writers by other English writers. The general editor of the series was the journalist, critic, politician, and supporter (and later biographer) of Gladstone, John Morley (1838–1923). The aim was to provide a short introduction to each subject and his works, but also that the life should illuminate the works, and vice versa. The subjects range chronologically from Chaucer to Thackeray and Dickens, and an important feature of the series is that many of the authors (Henry James on Hawthorne, Ward on Dickens) were discussing writers of the previous generation, and some (Trollope on Thackeray) had even known their subjects personally. The series exemplifies the British approach to literary biography and criticism at the end of the nineteenth century, and also reveals which authors were at that time regarded as canonical.

Sterne

Lawrence Sterne (1713–69) was an Anglican clergyman best remembered as the author of the satirical and highly influential novel *The Life and Opinions of Tristram Shandy, Gentleman*. After his ordination in 1738, Sterne led the life of a country vicar in Yorkshire, publishing a few satirical works before his masterpiece, which emerged in nine volumes between 1759 and 1767. The first two volumes were an immediate success, bringing him wealth, fame, and a place at the heart of contemporary English literary society. This work, published in the first series of English Men of Letters in 1882 by the journalist (and editor of Carlyle) Henry Duff Traill (1842–1900), provides a clear and informative biography. Drawing on Sterne's detailed letters to his daughter, Traill provides a fascinating account of Sterne's early life and his clerical career together with an analysis of his writing and influence upon English literature.

Cambridge University Press has long been a pioneer in the reissuing of out-of-print titles from its own backlist, producing digital reprints of books that are still sought after by scholars and students but could not be reprinted economically using traditional technology. The Cambridge Library Collection extends this activity to a wider range of books which are still of importance to researchers and professionals, either for the source material they contain, or as landmarks in the history of their academic discipline.

Drawing from the world-renowned collections in the Cambridge University Library, and guided by the advice of experts in each subject area, Cambridge University Press is using state-of-the-art scanning machines in its own Printing House to capture the content of each book selected for inclusion. The files are processed to give a consistently clear, crisp image, and the books finished to the high quality standard for which the Press is recognised around the world. The latest print-on-demand technology ensures that the books will remain available indefinitely, and that orders for single or multiple copies can quickly be supplied.

The Cambridge Library Collection will bring back to life books of enduring scholarly value (including out-of-copyright works originally issued by other publishers) across a wide range of disciplines in the humanities and social sciences and in science and technology.

Sterne

HENRY DUFF TRAILL

CAMBRIDGE
UNIVERSITY PRESS

CAMBRIDGE UNIVERSITY PRESS

Cambridge, New York, Melbourne, Madrid, Cape Town,
Singapore, São Paolo, Delhi, Tokyo, Mexico City

Published in the United States of America by Cambridge University Press, New York

www.cambridge.org
Information on this title: www.cambridge.org/9781108034524

© in this compilation Cambridge University Press 2011

This edition first published 1882
This digitally printed version 2011

ISBN 978-1-108-03452-4 Paperback

English Men of Letters

EDITED BY JOHN MORLEY

STERNE

STERNE

BY

H. D. TRAILL

London:
MACMILLAN AND CO.
1882.

PREFATORY NOTE.

THE materials for a biography of Sterne are by no means abundant. Of the earlier years of his life, the only existing record is that preserved in the brief autobiographical memoir which, a few months before his death, he composed, in the usual quaint *staccato* style of his familiar correspondence, for the benefit of his daughter. Of his childhood ; of his school days ; of his life at Cambridge, and in his Yorkshire Vicarage ; of his whole history in fact, up to the age of forty-six, we know nothing more than he has there jotted down. He attained that age in the year 1759 ; and at this date begins that series of his *Letters*, from which, for those who have the patience to sort them out of the chronological confusion in which his daughter and editress involved them, there is no doubt a good deal to be learnt. These letters, however, which extend down to 1768, the year of the writer's death, contain pretty nearly all the contemporary material that we have to depend on. Freely as Sterne mixed in the best literary society, there is singularly little to be gathered about him, even in the way of chance allusion and anecdote, from the memoirs and *ana* of his time. Of the many friends who would have been competent to write his biography while the facts were yet fresh, but one, John Wilkes, ever entertained—if he did seriously entertain—the idea of performing this pious work ; and he, in spite of the entreaties of Sterne's widow and daughter, then in straitened circumstances, left unredeemed his promise to do so. The brief memoir by Sir Walter Scott, which is prefixed to many popular editions of *Tristram Shandy* and the *Sentimental Journey*, sets out the so-called autobiography in full, but for the rest is mainly critical; Thackeray's well-known lecture-essay is almost wholly so; and nothing, worthy to be dignified by the name of a *Life of Sterne*, seems ever to have been published, until the appearance of Mr. Percy Fitzgerald's two stout volumes, under this title, some eighteen years ago. Of this work it is hardly too much to say, that it contains (no doubt with the admixture of a good deal of superfluous matter) nearly all the information as to the facts of Sterne's life that is now ever likely to be recovered. The evidence for certain of its statements of fact is not as thoroughly sifted as it might have been; and with some of its criticism I at least am unable to agree. But no one interested in the subject of this memoir can be insensible of his obligations to Mr. Fitzgerald, for the fruitful diligence with which he has laboured in a too long neglected field.

H. D. T.

BICKLEY, *May*, 1882.

CONTENTS.

CHAPTER VII.

CHAPTER VIII.

CHAPTER IX.

CHAPTER X.

CHAPTER XI.

STERNE.

CHAPTER I.

BIRTH, PARENTAGE, AND EARLY YEARS.

(1713—1724.)

TOWARDS the close of the month of November, 1713, one of the last of the English regiments which had been detained in Flanders to supervise the execution of the treaty of Utrecht, arrived at Clonmel from Dunkirk. The day after its arrival the regiment was disbanded ; and yet a few days later, on the 24th of the month, the wife of one of its subalterns gave birth to a son. The child who thus early displayed the perversity of his humour by so inopportune an appearance was LAURENCE STERNE. " My birthday," he says in the slipshod, loosely-strung notes by which he has been somewhat grandiloquently said to have " anticipated the labours " of the biographer—" my birthday was ominous to my poor father, who was the day after our arrival, with many other brave officers, broke and sent adrift into the wide world with a wife and two children."

Roger Sterne, however, now late ensign of the 34th or Chudleigh's regiment of foot, was after all in less evil case than were many probably of his comrades. He had kinsmen to whom he could look for at any rate temporary assistance, and his mother was a wealthy widow. The Sternes, originally of a Suffolk stock, had passed from that county to Nottinghamshire, and thence into York-shire, and were at this time a family of position and sub-stance in the last-named county. Roger's grandfather had been Archbishop of York, and a man of more note, if only through the accident of the times upon which he fell, than most of the incumbents of that see. He had played an exceptionally energetic part even for a Cavalier prelate in the great political struggle of the seventeenth century, and had suffered with fortitude and dignity in the royal cause. He had, moreover, a further claim to distinction in having been treated with common gratitude at the Restoration by the son of the monarch whom he had served. As Master of Jesus College, Cambridge, he had " been active in sending the University plate to his Majesty," and for this offence he was seized by Cromwell and carried in military custody to London, whence, after undergoing im-prisonment in various gaols, and experiencing other forms of hardship, he was at length permitted to retire to an obscure retreat in the country, there to commune with himself until that tyranny should be overpast. On the return of the exiled Stuarts Dr. Sterne was made Bishop of Carlisle, and a few years later was translated to the see of York. He lived to the age of eighty-six, and so far justified Burnet's accusation against him of " minding chiefly enriching himself," that he seems to have divided no fewer than four landed estates among his children. One of these, Simon Sterne, a younger son of the arch-bishop, himself married an heiress, the daughter of Sir Roger Jaques of Elvington ̦ and Roger, the father of

Laurence Sterne, was the seventh and youngest of the issue of this marriage. At the time when the double misfortune above recorded befell him at the hands of Lucina and the War Office, his father had been some years dead ; but Simon Sterne's widow was still mistress of the property which she had brought with her at her marriage, and to Elvington accordingly, "as soon," writes Sterne, "as I was able to be carried," the compulsorily retired ensign betook himself with his wife and his two children. He was not, however, compelled to remain long dependent on his mother. The ways of the military authorities were as inscrutable to the army of that day as they are in our day to our own. Before a year had passed the regiment was ordered to be re-established, and "our household decamped with bag and baggage for Dublin." This was in the autumn of 1714, and from that time onward for some eleven years the movements and fortunes of the Sterne family, as detailed in the narrative of its most famous member, form a history in which the ludicrous struggles strangely with the pathetic.

A husband, condemned to be the Ulysses-like plaything of adverse gods at the War Office ; an indefatigably prolific wife ; a succession of weak and ailing children ; misfortune in the seasons of journeying ; misfortune in the moods of the weather by sea and land—under all this combination of hostile chances and conditions was the struggle to be carried on. The little household was perpetually "on the move"—a little household which was always becoming and never remaining bigger—continually increased by births, only to be again reduced by deaths— until the contest between the deadly hardships of travel and the fatal fecundity of Mrs. Sterne was brought by events to a natural close. Almost might the unfortunate

lady have exclaimed, *Quæ regio in terris nostri non plena
laboris ?* She passes from Ireland to England, and from
England to Ireland, from inland garrison to sea-port town
and back again, incessantly bearing and incessantly burying
children—until even her son in his narrative begins to speak
of losing one infant at this place, and "leaving another
behind" on that journey, almost as if they were so many
overlooked or misdirected articles of luggage. The tragic
side of the history, however, overshadows the grotesque.
When we think how hard a business was travel even
under the most favourable conditions in those days, and
how serious even in our own times, when travel is easy,
are the discomforts of the women and children of a regiment on the march—we may well pity these unresting
followers of the drum. As to Mrs. Sterne herself, she
seems to have been a woman of a pretty tough fibre, and
she came moreover of a campaigning stock. Her father
was a "noted suttler" of the name of Nuttle, and her first
husband—for she was a widow when Roger Sterne married
her—had been a soldier also. She had, therefore, served
some years apprenticeship to the military life before these
wanderings began ; and she herself was destined to live
to a good old age. But somehow or other she failed to
endow her offspring with her own robust constitution and
powers of endurance. "My father's children were," as
Laurence Sterne grimly puts it, "not made to last long ;"
but one cannot help suspecting that it was the hardships of
those early years which carried them off in their infancy
with such painful regularity and despatch, and that it was
to the same cause that their surviving brother owed the
beginnings of that fatal malady by which his own life was
cut short.

The diary of their travels—for the early part of

Sterne's memoirs amounts to scarcely more—is the more effective for its very brevity and abruptness. Save for one interval of somewhat longer sojourn than usual at Dublin, the reader has throughout it all the feeling of the traveller who never finds time to unpack his portmanteau. On the re-enrolment of the regiment in 1714, "our household," says the narrative, "decamped from York with bag and baggage for Dublin. Within a month my father left us, being ordered to Exeter; where, in a sad winter, my mother and her two children followed him, travelling from Liverpool, by land, to Plymouth." At Plymouth, Mrs. Sterne gave birth to a son, christened Joram; and, "in twelve months' time we were all sent back to Dublin. My mother," with her three children, "took ship at Bristol for Ireland, and had a narrow escape from being cast away by a leak springing up in the vessel. At length, after many perils and struggles, we got to Dublin." Here intervenes the short breathing-space, of which mention has been made—an interval employed by Roger Sterne in "spending a great deal of money" on a "large house," which he hired and furnished; and then "in the year one thousand seven hundred and nineteen, all unhinged again." The regiment had been ordered off to the Isle of Wight, thence to embark for Spain, on "the Vigo Expedition," and "we," who accompanied it, "were driven into Milford Haven, but afterwards landed at Bristol, and thence by land to Plymouth again, and to the Isle of Wight;" losing on this expedition "poor Joram, a pretty boy, who died of the small-pox." In the Isle of Wight, Mrs. Sterne and her family remained, till the Vigo Expedition returned home; and during her stay there "poor Joram's loss was supplied by the birth of a girl, Anne," a "pretty blossom," but destined to fall "at the age of three years." On the return of the regiment to Wicklow, Roger Sterne again sent to collect his family round him. " We embarked for Dublin, and had all been cast away by a most violent storm ; but, through the intercession of my mother, the captain was prevailed upon to turn back into Wales, where we stayed a month, and at length got into Dublin, and travelled by land to Wicklow, where my father had, for some weeks, given us over for lost." Here a year passed, and another child, Devijeher—so called after the Colonel of the regiment—was born. " From thence we decamped to stay half a year with Mr. Fetherston, a clergyman, about seven miles from Wicklow, who, being a relative of my mother's, invited us to his parsonage at Animo.[1] From thence, again, " we followed the regiment to Dublin," where again "we lay in the barracks a year." In 1722 the regiment was ordered to Carrickfergus. " We all decamped, but got no further than Drogheda ; thence ordered to Mullingar, forty miles west, where, by Provi- dence, we stumbled upon a kind relation, a collateral

---

[1] "It was in this parish," says Sterne, " that I had that won- derful escape in falling through a mill race while the mill was going, and being taken up unhurt; the story is incredible, but known to all that part of Ireland where hundreds of the common people flocked to see me." More incredible still does it seem that Thoresby should relate the occurrence of an accident of precisely the same kind to Sterne's great-grandfather the Archbishop. " Playing near a mill, he fell within a claw ; there was but one board or bucket wanting in the whole wheel, but a gracious Pro- vidence so ordered it that the void place came down at that moment, else he had been crushed to death ; but was reserved to be a grand benefactor afterwards." (Thoresby, ii. 15.) But what will pro- bably strike the reader as more extraordinary even than this coincidence is that Sterne should have been either unaware of it, or should have omitted mention of it in the above passage.

descendant from Archbishop Sterne, who took us all to
his castle, and kindly entertained us for a year." Thence,
by "a most rueful journey" to Carrickfergus, where "we
arrived in six or seven days." Here, at the age of three,
little Devijeher obtained a happy release from his name.;
and "another child, Susan, was sent to fill his place, who
also left us behind in this weary journey." In the
"autumn of this year, or the spring of the next"—
Sterne's memory failing in exactitude at the very point
where we should have expected it to be most precise—
"my father obtained permission of his colonel to fix me
at school;" and henceforth the boy's share in the family
wanderings was at an end. But his father had yet to be
ordered from Carrickfergus to Londonderry, where at last
a permanent child, Catherine, was born ; and .thence to
Gibraltar, to take part in the Defence of that famous
Rock, where the much-enduring campaigner was run
through the body in a duel, " about a goose " (a thoroughly
Shandian catastrophe) ; and thence to Jamaica, where,
" with a constitution impaired " by the sword-thrust,
earned in his anserine quarrel, he was defeated in a more
deadly duel with the "country fever," and died. " His
malady," writes his son, with a touch of feeling struggling
through his dislocated grammar, " took away his senses
first, and made a child of him ; and then in a month
or two walking about continually without complaining,
till the moment he sat down in an arm-chair and breathed
his last."

There is, as has been observed, a certain mixture of the
comic and the pathetic in the life-history of this obscure
father of a famous son. His life was clearly not a
fortunate one, so far as external circumstances go ; but its
misfortunes had no sort of consoling dignity about them.

Roger Sterne's lot in the world was not so much an
unhappy as an uncomfortable one ; and discomfort earns
little sympathy, and absolutely no admiration, for its
sufferers.   He somehow reminds us of one of those Irish
heroes—good-natured, peppery, debt-loaded, light-hearted,
shiftless—whose fortunes we follow with mirthful and
half-contemptuous sympathy in the pages of Thackeray.
He was obviously a typical specimen of that class of men
who are destitute alike of the virtues and failings of the
" respectable " and successful ; whom many people love
and no one respects ; whom everybody pities in their
struggles and difficulties, but whom few pity without a
smile.

It is evident, however, that he succeeded in winning the
affection of one who had not too much affection of the
deeper kind to spare for any one.   The figure of Roger
Sterne alone stands out with any clearness by the side of
the ceaselessly flitting mother and phantasmal children of
Laurence Sterne's Memoir ; and it is touched in with
strokes so vivid and characteristic that critics have been
tempted to find in it the original of the most famous
portrait in the Shandy gallery.   " My father," says
Sterne, " was a little smart man, active to the last degree
in all exercises, most patient of fatigue and disappoint-
ments, of which it pleased God to give him full measure.
He was, in his temper, somewhat rapid and hasty, but of
a kindly sweet disposition, void of all design, and so
innocent in his own intentions, that he suspected no one ;
so that you might have cheated him ten times a day, if
nine had not been sufficient for your purpose."   This is a
captivating little picture ; and it no doubt presents traits
which may have impressed themselves early and deeply
on the imagination which was afterwards to give birth to

" My Uncle Toby." The simplicity of nature and the
" kindly sweet disposition " are common to both the
ensign of real life and to the immortal Captain Shandy
of fiction ; but the criticism which professes to find traces
of Roger Sterne's " rapid and hasty temper " in my Uncle
Toby, is compelled to strain itself considerably. And,
on the whole, there seems no reason to believe that Sterne
borrowed more from the character of his father than any
writer must necessarily, and perhaps unconsciously, borrow
from his observation of the moral and mental qualities of
those with whom he has come into most frequent contact.

That Laurence Sterne passed the first eleven years of
his life with such an exemplar of these simple virtues of
kindliness, guilelessness and courage ever before him, is
perhaps the best that can be said for the lot in which his
early days were cast. In almost all other respects there
could hardly have been—for a quick-witted, precocious,
imitative boy—a worse bringing-up. No one, I should
imagine, ever more needed discipline in his youth than
Sterne ; and the camp is a place of discipline for the
soldier only. To all others whom necessity attaches to
it, and to the young especially, it is rather a school of
licence and irregularity. It is fair to remember these
disadvantages of Sterne's early training, in judging of the
many defects as a man, and laxities as a writer, which
marked his later life : though, on the other hand, there is
no denying the reality and value of some of the counter-
vailing advantages which came to him from his boyish
surroundings. The conception of my Uncle Toby need
not have been taken whole from Roger Sterne, or from
any one actual captain of a marching regiment ; but the
constant sight of, and converse with, many captains and

many corporals may undoubtedly have contributed much
to the vigour and vitality of Toby Shandy and Corporal
Trim.   So far as the externals of portraiture were concerned, there can be no doubt that his art benefited much
from his early military life.   His soldiers have the true
stamp of the soldier about them in air and language ; and
when his captain and corporal fight their Flemish battles
over again, we are thoroughly conscious that we are
listening, under the dramatic form, to one who must
himself have heard many a chapter of the same splendid
story from the lips of the very men who had helped to
break the pride of the Grand Monarque under Marlborough
and Eugene.

CHAPTER II.

(1723—1738.)

IT was not—as we have seen from the Memoir—till the autumn of 1723, "or the spring of the following year," that Roger Sterne obtained leave of his colonel to "fix" his son at school; and this would bring Laurence to the tolerably advanced age of ten, before beginning his education in any systematic way. He records, under date of 1721, that "in this year I learned to write, &c. ;" but it is not probable that the " &c."—that indolent symbol of which Sterne makes such irritating use in all his familiar writing—covers, in this case, any wide extent of educational advance. The boy, most likely, could just read and write, and no more, at the time when he was fixed at school, " near Halifax, with an able master :" a judicious selection, no doubt, both of place as well as teacher. Mr. Fitzgerald, to whose researches we owe as much light as is ever likely to be thrown upon this obscure and probably not very interesting period of Sterne's life, has pointed out that Richard Sterne, eldest son of the late Simon Sterne, and uncle, therefore, of Laurence, was one of the governors of Halifax Grammar School, and that he may have used his interest to obtain his nephew's admission to the foundation as the grandson of a Halifax

man, and so, constructively, a child of the parish. But
be this as it may, it is more than probable that from the
time when he was sent to Halifax School, the whole care
and cost of the boy's education was borne by his Yorkshire relatives. The memoir says that, " by God's care of
me, my cousin Sterne, of Elvington, became a father to
me, and sent me to the University, &c. &c. :" and it is
to be inferred from this that the benevolent guardianship of Sterne's uncle Richard (who died in 1732, the
year before Laurence was admitted of Jesus College,
Cambridge,) must have been taken up by his son. Of
his school course—though it lasted for over seven years,
the autobiographer has little to say ; nothing, indeed,
except that he " cannot omit mentioning " that anecdote
with which everybody, I suppose, who has ever come
across the briefest notice of Sterne's life, is familiar.
The schoolmaster " had the ceiling of the schoolroom
new-whitewashed, and the ladder remained there. I, one
unlucky day, mounted it, and wrote with a brush in large
capital letters, LAU. STERNE, for which the usher
severely whipped me. My master was very much hurt at
this, and said before me that never should that name be
effaced, for I was a boy of genius, and he was sure I
should come to preferment. This expression made me
forget the blows I had received." It is hardly to be
supposed, of course, that this story is pure romance ; but
it is difficult, on the other hand, to believe that the
incident has been related by Sterne exactly as it happened. That the recorded prediction may have been
made in jest—or even in earnest (for penetrating teachers
have these prophetic moments sometimes)—is, of course,
possible ; but that Sterne's master was " very much hurt "
at the boy's having been justly punished for an act of

wanton mischief, or that he recognized it as the natural
privilege of nascent genius to deface newly whitewashed
ceilings must have been a delusion of the humourist's
later years. The extreme fatuity which it would compel
us to attribute to the schoolmaster seems inconsistent
with the power of detecting intellectual capacity in any
one else. On the whole, one inclines to suspect that the
remark belonged to that order of half sardonic, half
kindly jest which a certain sort of pedagogue sometimes
throws off, for the consolation of a recently-caned boy;
and that Sterne's vanity, either then or afterwards (for
it remained juvenile all his life), translated it into a serious
prophecy. In itself, however, the urchin's freak was only
too unhappily characteristic of the man. The trick of
befouling what was clean (and because it was clean)
clung to him most tenaciously all his days ; and many a
fair white surface—of humour, of fancy, or of sentiment
—was to be disfigured by him in after-years with stains
and splotches in which we can all too plainly decipher
the literary signature of Laurence Sterne.

At Halifax School the boy, as has been said, remained
for about eight years : that is, until he was nearly nineteen,
and for some months after his father's death at Port
Antonio, which occurred in March, 1731. "In the
year '32," says the memoir, "my cousin sent me to the
University, where I stayed some time." In the course of
his first year he read for and obtained a sizarship, to
which the college records show that he was duly admitted on the 6th of July, 1733. The selection of Jesus
College was a natural one : Sterne's great-grandfather,
the afterwards Archbishop, had been its Master, and had
founded scholarships there, to one of which the young
sizar was, a year after his admission, elected. No in-

ference can, of course, be drawn from this as to Sterne's
proficiency, or even industry, in his academical studies:
it is scarcely more than a testimony to the fact of decent
and regular behaviour. He was *bene natus*, in the sense
of being related to the right man, the Founder; and in
those days he need be only very *modicè doctus* indeed, in
order to qualify himself for admission to the enjoyment
of his kinsman's benefactions. Still he must have been
orderly and well-conducted in his ways: and this he
would also seem to have been, from the fact of his
having passed through his University course without any
apparent break or hitch, and having been admitted to his
Bachelor's degree after no more than the normal period
of residence. The only remark which, in the Memoir, he
vouchsafes to bestow upon his academical career, is, that
" 'twas there that I commenced a friendship with Mr.
H——, which has been lasting on both sides:" and it
may perhaps be said that this *was*, from one point of
view, the most important event of his Cambridge life.
For Mr. H—— was John Hall, afterwards John Hall
Stevenson, the " Eugenius" of *Tristram Shandy;* the
master of Skelton Castle, at which Sterne was, throughout
life, to be a frequent and most familiar visitor; and,
unfortunately, also a person whose later reputation, both
as a man and a writer, became such as seriously to com-
promise the not very robust respectability of his clerical
comrade. Sterne and Hall were distant cousins and it
may have been the tie of consanguinity which first drew
them together. But there was evidently a thorough con-
geniality of the most unlucky sort between them; and
from their first meeting as undergraduates at Jesus, until
the premature death of the elder, they continued to supply each other's minds with precisely that sort of occupation

and stimulus of which each by the grace of nature stood
least in need. That their close intimacy was ill-calculated
to raise Sterne's reputation in later years may be inferred
from the fact that Hall Stevenson afterwards obtained
literary notoriety by the publication of *Crazy Tales*, a
collection of comic but extremely broad ballads in which
his clerical friend was quite unjustly suspected of having
had a hand. Mr. Hall was also reported, whether truly or
falsely, to have been a member of Wilkes's famous confra-
ternity of Medmenham Abbey; and from this it was an
easy step for gossip to advance to the assertion that the
Rev. Mr. Sterne had himself been admitted to that unholy
order.

Among acquaintances which the young sizar of Jesus
might have more profitably made at Cambridge, but did
not, was that of a student destined, like himself, to leave
behind him a name famous in English letters. Gray,
born three years later than Sterne, had entered a year
after him at Cambridge as a pensioner of Peterhouse, and
the two students went through their terms together,
though the poet at the time took no degree. There was
probably little enough in common between the shy,
fastidious, slightly effeminate pensioner of Peterhouse, and
a scholar of Jesus, whose chief friend and comrade was a
man like Hall; and no close intimacy between the two
men, if they had come across each other, would have been
very likely to arise. But it does not appear that they
could have ever met or heard of each other, for Gray
writes of Sterne, after *Tristram Shandy* had made him
famous, in terms which clearly show that he did not
recall his fellow-undergraduate.

In January, 1736, Sterne took his B.A. degree, and
quitted Cambridge for York, where another of his father's

brothers now makes his appearance as his patron. Dr.
Jacques Sterne was the second son of Simon Sterne, of
Elvington, and a man apparently of more marked and
vigorous character than any of his brothers. What
induced him now to take notice of the nephew, whom in
boyhood and early youth he had left to the unshared
guardianship of his brother, and brother's son, does not
appear; but the personal history of this energetic pluralist
—Prebendary of Durham, Archdeacon of Cleveland,
Canon Residentiary, Precentor, Prebendary, and Archdeacon of York, Rector of Rise, and Rector of Hornsey-
cum-Riston—suggests the surmise that he detected
qualities in the young Cambridge graduate which would
make him useful. For Dr. Sterne was a typical specimen
of the Churchman-politician, in days when both com-
ponents of the compound word meant a good deal more
than they do now. The Archdeacon was a devoted Whig,
a Hanoverian to the backbone; and he held it his duty
to support the Protestant succession, not only by the
spiritual but by the secular arm. He was a great
electioneerer, as befitted times when the claims of two
rival dynasties virtually met upon the hustings, and he
took a prominent part in the great Yorkshire contest
of the year 1734. His most vigorous display of energy,
however, was made, as was natural, in "the '45." The
Whig Archdeacon, not then Archdeacon of the East
Riding, nor as yet quite buried under the mass of preferments which he afterwards accumulated, seems to have
thought that this indeed was the crisis of his fortunes, and
that unless he was prepared to die a mere prebendary,
canon, and rector of one or two benefices, now was the
time to strike a blow for his advancement in the Church.
His bustling activity at this trying time was indeed

portentous, and at last took the form of arresting the
unfortunate Dr. Burton (the original of Dr.
Slop) on suspicion of holding communication with the invading
army of the Pretender, then on its march southward from
Edinburgh. The suspect, who was wholly innocent, was
taken to London and kept in custody for nearly a year
before being discharged, after which, by way of a slight
redress, a letter of reprimand for his *trop de zèle* was sent
by direction of Lord Carteret to the militant dignitary.
But the desired end was nevertheless attained, and Dr.
Sterne suceeeded in crowning the edifice of his ecclesiastical
honours.[1]

There can be little doubt that patronage extended by
such an uncle to such a nephew, received its full equivalent
in some way or other, and indeed the Memoir gives us a
clue to the mode in which payment was made. "My
uncle," writes Sterne, describing their subsequent rupture,
" quarrelled with me because I would not write paragraphs
in the newspapers ; though he was a party-man, I was
not, and detested such dirty work, thinking it beneath
me. From that time he became my bitterest enemy."
The date of this quarrel cannot be precisely fixed; but
we gather from an autograph letter (now in the British

---

[1] A once-familiar piece of humorous verse describes the upset
of a coach containing a clerical pluralist,—

> When struggling on the ground was seen
> A Rector, Vicar, Canon, Dean ;
> You might have thought the coach was full,
> But no ! 'twas only Dr. Bull.

Dr. Jacques Sterne, however, might have been thrown out of one
of the more capacious vehicles of the London General Omnibus
Company, with almost the same misleading effect upon those who
only *heard* of the mishap.

Museum) from Sterne to Archdeacon Blackburne that by
the year 1750 the two men had for some time ceased to
be on friendly terms. Probably, however, the breach
occurred subsequently to the rebellion of '45, and it may
be that it arose out of the excess of partisan zeal which
Dr. Sterne developed in that year, and which his nephew
very likely did not in his opinion sufficiently share. But
this is quite consistent with the younger man's having
up to that time assisted the elder in his party polemics. He
certainly speaks in his "Letters" of his having "employed
his brains for an ungrateful person," and the remark is
made in a way and in a connexion which seems to imply
that the services rendered to his uncle were mainly
literary. If so his declaration that he "would not write
paragraphs in the newspapers," can only mean that he would
not go on writing them.   Be this as it may, however, it is
certain that the Archdeacon for some time found his
account in maintaining friendly relations with his
nephew, and that during that period he undoubtedly did
a good deal for his advancement.   Sterne was ordained
deacon by the Bishop of Lincoln in March, 1736, only
three months after taking his B.A. degree, and took priest's
orders in August, 1738, whereupon his uncle immediately
obtained for him the living of Sutton-on-the-Forest, into
which he was inducted a few days afterwards.   Other
preferments followed, to be noted hereafter, and it must be
admitted that until the quarrel occurred about the "party
paragraphs" the Archdeacon did his duty by his
nephew after the peculiar fashion of that time.   When
that quarrel came, however, it seems to have snapped
more ties than one, for in the Memoir Sterne speaks of
his youngest sister Catherine as "still living, but most
unhappily estranged from me by my uncle's wickedness

and her own folly." Of his elder sister Mary, who was
born at Lille a year before himself, he records that "she
married one Weemans in Dublin, who used her most
unmercifully, spent his substance, became a bankrupt,
and left my poor sister to shift for herself, which she was
able to do but for a few months, for she went to a friend's
house in the country and died of a broken heart." Truly
an unlucky family.[2] Only three to survive the hardships
among which the years of their infancy were passed, and
this to be the history of two out of the three survivors!

---

[2] The mother, Mrs. Sterne, makes her appearance once more
for a moment in or about the year 1758. Horace Walpole, and
after him Byron, accused Sterne of having "preferred whining over
a dead ass to relieving a living mother," and the former went so
far as to declare "on indubitable authority" that Mrs. Sterne,
"who kept a school (in Ireland), having run in debt on account of
an extravagant daughter, would have rotted in a gaol if the parents
of her scholars had not raised a subscription for her." Even "the
indubitable authority," however, does not positively assert—whatever may be meant to be insinuated—that Sterne himself did nothing to assist his mother, and Mr. Fitzgerald justly points out
that to pay the *whole* debts of a bankrupt school might well have
been beyond a Yorkshire clergyman's means. Anyhow there is
evidence that Sterne at a later date than this was actively concern-
ing himself about his mother's interests. She afterwards came to
York, whither he went to meet her; and he then writes to a friend,
"I trust my poor mother's affair is by this time ended to *our*
comfort and hers."

CHAPTER III.

(1738—1759.)

GREAT writers who spring late and suddenly from obscurity into fame and yet die early, must always form more or less perplexing subjects of literary biography. The processes of their intellectual and artistic growth lie hidden in nameless years: their genius is not revealed to the world until it has reached its full maturity, and many aspects of it which perhaps would have easily explained themselves if the gradual development had gone on before men's eyes, remain often unexplained to the last. By few, if any, of the more celebrated English men of letters is this observation so forcibly illustrated as it is in the case of Sterne: the obscure period of his life so greatly exceeded in duration the brief season of his fame, and its obscurity was so exceptionally profound. He was forty-seven years of age when, at a bound, he achieved celebrity; he was not five-and-fifty when he died. And though it might be too much to say that the artist sprang, like the reputation, full-grown into being, it is nevertheless true that there are no marks of positive immaturity to be detected even in the earliest public displays of his art. His work grows indeed most marvellously in vividness and symmetry as he proceeds, but there are no visible signs of growth in the

workman's skill. Even when the highest point of finish
is attained, we cannot say that the hand is any more
cunning than it was from the first. As well might we say
that the last light touches of the sculptor's chisel upon the
perfected statue are more skilful, than its first vigorous
strokes upon the shapeless block.

It is certain, however, that Sterne must have been
storing up his material of observation, secreting his reflections on life and character, and consciously or unconsciously
maturing his powers of expression during the whole of
those silent twenty years which have now to be passed
under brief review. With one exception, to be noted
presently, the only known writings of his which belong
to this period are sermons, and these—a mere "scratch"
collection of pulpit discourses which as soon as he had
gained the public ear, he hastened in characteristic fashion
to rummage from his desk and carry to the book-market—
throw no light upon the problem before us. There are
sermons of Sterne which alike in manner and matter dis-
close the author of *Tristram Shandy;* but they are not
among those which he preached or wrote before that work
was given to the world. They are not its ancestors but
its descendants. They belong to the post-Shandian period,
and are in obvious imitation of the Shandian style; while
in none of the earlier ones—not even in that famous
homily on a Good Conscience, which did not succeed till
Corporal Trim preached it before the brothers Shandy and
Dr. Slop—can we trace either the trick of style or the
turn of thought that give piquancy to the novel. Yet
the peculiar qualities of mind, and the special faculty of
workmanship of which this turn of thought and trick of
style were the product, must of course have been poten-
tially present from the beginning. Men do not blossom

forth as wits, humourists, masterly delineators of character, and skilful performers on a highly-strung and carefully-tuned sentimental instrument all at once, after entering their "forties;" and the only wonder is that a possessor of these powers—some of them of the kind which, as a rule and in most men, seeks almost as irresistibly for exercise as even the poetic instinct itself—should have been held so long unemployed.

There is, however, one very common stimulus to literary exertions which in Sterne's case was undoubtedly wanting—a superabundance of unoccupied time. We have little reason, it is true, to suppose that this light-minded and valetudinarian Yorkshire parson was at any period of his life an industrious "parish-priest;" but it is probable nevertheless that time never hung very heavily upon his hands. In addition to the favourite amusements which he enumerates in the Memoir, he was all his days addicted to one which is perhaps the most absorbing of all— flirtation. Philandering, and especially philandering of the Platonic and ultra-sentimental order, is almost the one human pastime of which its votaries never seem to tire ; and its constant ministrations to human vanity may serve perhaps to account for their unwearied absorption in its pursuit. Sterne's first love-affair—an affair of which unfortunately the consequences were more lasting than the passion—took place immediately upon his leaving Cambridge. To relate it as he relates it to his daughter : "At York I became acquainted with your mother, and courted her for two years. She owned she liked me, but thought herself not rich enough or me too poor to be joined together. She went to her sister's in S[taffordshire], and I wrote to her often. I believe then she was partly determined to have me, but would not say so. At her return

she fell into a consumption, and one evening that I was
sitting by her with an almost broken heart to see her so
ill, she said : ' My dear Laury, I never can be yours, for
I verily believe I have not long to live ! but I have left
you every shilling of my fortune.' Upon that she showed
me her will. This generosity overpowered me. It pleased
God that she recovered, and we were married in 1741."
The name of this lady was Elizabeth Lumley, and it was
to her that Sterne addressed those earliest letters which
his daughter included in the collection published by her
some eight years after her father's death. They were added,
the preface tells us, " in justice to Mr. Sterne's delicate feelings ;" and in our modern usage of the word " delicate,"
as equivalent to infirm of health and probably short of
life, they no doubt do full justice to the passion which
they are supposed to express. It would be unfair of
course to judge any love-letters of that period by the
standard of sincerity applied in our own less artificial age.
All such compositions seem frigid and formal enough to
us of to-day ; yet in most cases of genuine attachment we
usually find at least a sentence here and there in which the
natural accents of the heart make themselves heard above
the affected modulations of the style. But the letters of
Sterne's courtship maintain the pseudo-poetic, shepherd-
and-shepherdess strain throughout ; or if the lover ever
abandons it, it is only to make somewhat maudlin record
of those " tears " which flowed a little too easily at all times
throughout his life. These letters, however, have a certain critical interest in their bearing upon those sensibilities which Sterne afterwards learned to cultivate in
a forcing-frame, with a view to the application of their
produce to the purposes of an art of pathetic writing
which simulates nature with such admirable fidelity at

its best, and descends to such singular bathos at its
worst.

The marriage preluded by this courtship did not take
place till Sterne had already been three years vicar of
Sutton-on-the-Forest, the benefice which had been procured for him by his uncle the archdeacon; through
whose interest also he was appointed successively to
two prebends—preferments which were less valuable to
him for their emolument than for the ecclesiastical
status which they conferred upon him, for the excuse
which they gave him for periodical visits to the cathe-
dral city to fulfil the residential conditions of his offices,
and for the opportunity thus afforded him of mixing in
and studying the society of the Close. Upon his
union with Miss Lumley, and, in a somewhat curious
fashion, by her means, he obtained in addition the living
of Stillington. " A friend of hers in the south had promised her that if she married a clergyman in Yorkshire,
when the living became vacant he would make her a
compliment of it ; " and made accordingly this singular
" compliment " was. At Sutton Sterne remained nearly
twenty years doing duty at both places, during which
time " books, painting, fiddling, and shooting were," he
says, "my chief amusements." With what success he
shot, and with what skill he fiddled, we know not. His
writings contain not a few musical metaphors and allusions
to music, which seem to indicate a competent acquaintance with its technicalities ; but the specimen of his powers
as an artist, which Mr. Fitzgerald has reproduced from
his illustrations of a volume of poems by Mr. Woodhull,
does not dispose one to rate highly his proficiency in this
accomplishment. We may expect that after all it was the
first-mentioned of his amusements in which he took the

greatest delight, and that neither the brush, the bow, nor
the fowling-piece was nearly so often in his hand as the
book. Within a few miles of Sutton, at Skelton Castle,
an almost unique Roman stronghold since modernized by
Gothic hands, dwelt his college-friend John Hall Stevenson, whose well-stocked library contained a choice but
heterogeneous collection of books—old French " ana," and
the learning of mediæval doctors—books intentionally and
books unintentionally comic, the former of which Sterne
read with an only too retentive a memory for their jests,
and the latter with an acutely humorous appreciation of
their solemn trifling.   Later on it will be time to note the
extent to which he utilized these results of his widely dis-
cursive reading, and to examine the legitimacy of the
mode in which he used them: here it is enough to say
generally that the materials for many a burlesque chapter
of *Tristram Shandy* must have been unconsciously storing
themselves in his mind in many an amused hour passed
by Sterne in the library of Skelton Castle.

But before finally quitting this part of my subject it
may be as well perhaps to deal somewhat at length with
a matter which will doubtless have to be many times
incidentally referred to in the course of this study, but
which I now hope to relieve myself from the necessity of
doing more than touch upon hereafter.   I refer of course
to Sterne's perpetually recurring flirtations.   This is a
matter almost as impossible to omit from any biography
of Sterne, as it would be to omit it from any biography
of Goethe.   The English humourist did not, it is true,
engage in the pastime in the serious, not to say scientific
spirit of the German philosopher-poet; it was not deliberately made by the former as by the latter to
contribute to his artistic development ; but it is neverthe-

less hardly open to doubt that Sterne's philandering
propensities did exercise an influence upon his literary
character and work in more ways than one.   That his
marriage was an ill-assorted and unhappy union was
hardly so much the cause of his inconstancy as its effect.
It may well be, of course, that the "dear L." whose
moral and mental graces her lover had celebrated in such
superfine sentimental fashion, was a commonplace person
enough.   That she was really a woman of the exquisite
stolidity of Mrs. Shandy, and that her exasperating feats
as an *assentatrix* did, as has been suggested, supply the
model for the irresistibly ludicrous colloquies between
the philosopher and his wife, there is no sufficient warrant
for believing.   But it is quite possible that the daily
companion of one of the most indefatigable jesters that
ever lived may have been unable to see a joke; that she
regarded her husband's wilder drolleries as mere horse-
collar grimacing, and that the point of his subtler humour
escaped her altogether.   But even if it were so, it is, to
say the least of it, doubtful whether Sterne suffered at all
on this ground from the wounded feelings of the *mari
incompris*, while it is next to certain that it does not need
the sting of any such disappointment to account for his
alienation.   He must have had plenty of time and opportunity to discover Miss Lumley's intellectual limitations
during the two years of his courtship; and it is not
likely that even if they were as well marked as Mrs.
Shandy's own, they would have done much of themselves
to estrange the couple.   Sympathy is not the necessity to
the humourist which the poet finds, or imagines, it to be
to himself: the humourist indeed will sometimes contrive
to extract from the very absence of sympathy in those
about him a keener relish for his reflections.   With

sentiment, indeed, and still more with sentimentalism,
the case would of course be different; but as for Mr.
Sterne's demands for sympathy in that department of his
life and art, one may say without the least hesitation that
they would have been beyond the power of any one
woman, however distinguished a disciple of the "Laura
Matilda" school, to satisfy. "I must ever," he frankly
says in one of the "Yorick to Eliza" letters, "I must
ever have some Dulcinea in my head : it harmonizes the
soul;" and he might have added that he found it
impossible to sustain the harmony without frequently
changing the Dulcinea.   One may suspect that Mrs.
Sterne soon had cause for jealousy, and it is at least
certain that several years before Sterne's emergence into
notoriety their estrangement was complete.   One daughter
was born to them in 1745, but lived scarcely more than
long enough to be rescued from the *limbus infantium* by
the prompt rites of the Church.   The child was christened
Lydia, and died on the following day.   Its place was filled
in 1747 by a second daughter, also christened Lydia, who
lived to become the wife of M. de Medalle, and the
not very judicious editress of the posthumous "Letters."
For her as she grew up Sterne conceived a genuine and
truly fatherly affection, and it is in writing to her and of
her that we see him at his best ; or rather one might say
it is almost only then that we can distinguish the true
notes of the heart through that habitual falsetto of
sentimentalism, which distinguishes most of Sterne's communications with the other sex.   There was no subsequent
issue of the marriage, and from one of the letters most
indiscreetly included in Mdme. de Medalle's collection,
it is to be ascertained that some four years or so after
Lydia's birth the relations between Sterne and Mrs. Sterne

ceased to be conjugal, and never again resumed that character.

It is, however, probable upon the husband's own con-
fessions, that he had given his wife earlier cause for
jealousy, and certainly from the time when he begins to
reveal himself in correspondence there seems to be hardly
a moment when some such cause was not in existence—
in the person of this, that, or the other lackadaisical
damsel or coquettish matron. From Miss Fourmantelle,
the "dear, dear Kitty," to whom Sterne was making
violent love in 1759, the year of the York publication of
Tristram Shandy, down to Mrs. Draper, the heroine of
the famous "Yorick to Eliza" letters, the list of ladies
who seem to have kindled flames in that susceptible
breast is almost as long and more real than the roll of
mistresses immortalized by Horace. How Mrs. Sterne
at first bore herself under her husband's ostentatious
neglect, there is no direct evidence to show. That she
ultimately took refuge in indifference we can perceive,
but it is to be feared that she was not always able to
maintain the attitude of contemptuous composure. So at
least we may suspect from the evidence of that Frenchman
who met "le bon et agréable Tristram," and his wife, at
Montpellier, and who, characteristically sympathizing with
the inconstant husband, declared that his wife's incessant
pursuit of him made him pass "d'assez mauvais moments,"
which he bore "with the patience of an angel." But on
the whole Mrs. Sterne's conduct seems by her husband's
own admissions to have been not wanting in dignity.

As to the nature of Sterne's love-affairs I have come,
though not without hesitation, to the conclusion that they
were most, if not all of them, what is called, somewhat
absurdly, Platonic. In saying this, however, I am by no

means prepared to assert that they would all of them have
passed muster before a prosaic and uusentimental British
jury as mere indiscretions, and nothing worse. Sterne's
relations with Miss Fourmantelle, for instance, assumed
at last a profoundly compromising character, and it is far
from improbable that the worst construction would have
been put upon them by one of the plain-dealing tribunals
aforesaid. Certainly a young woman who leaves her
mother at York, and comes up to London to reside alone
in lodgings where she is constantly being visited by a
lover who is himself living *en garçon* in the metropolis,
can hardly complain if her imprudence is fatal to her reputation : neither can he if his own suffers in the same
way. But as I am not of those who hold that the con-
ventionally " innocent " is the equivalent of the morally
harmless in this matter, I cannot regard the question as
worth any very minute investigation. I am not sure that
the habitual male flirt, who neglects his wife to sit continually languishing at the feet of some other woman,
gives much less pain and scandal to others, or does much
less mischief to himself and the objects of his adoration,
than the thorough-going profligate ; and I even feel
tempted to risk the apparent paradox, that from the artistic point of view, Sterne lost rather than gained by the
generally Platonic character of his amours. For, as it
was, the restraint of one instinct of his nature implied
the over-indulgence of another which stood in at least as
much need of chastenment. If his love-affairs stopped
short of the gratification of the senses, they involved a
perpetual fondling and caressing of those effeminate sen-
·sibilities of his into that condition of hyper-æsthesia
which, though Sterne regarded it as the strength, was in
reality the weakness, of his art.

Injurious, however, as was the effect which Sterne's philanderings exercised upon his personal and literary character, it is not likely that, at least at this period of his life at Sutton, they had in any degree compromised his reputation. For this he had provided in other ways, and principally by his exceedingly injudicious choice of associates. "As to the squire of the parish," he remarks in the memoir, " I cannot say we were on a very friendly footing, but at Stillington the family of the C[roft]s showed us every kindness : 'twas most agreeable to be within a mile and a half of an amiable family who were ever cordial friends ;" and who, it may be added, appear to have been Sterne's only reputable acquaintances. For the satisfaction of all other social needs he seems to have resorted to a companionship which it was hardly possible for a clergyman to frequent without scandal—that, namely, of John Hall Stevenson and the kindred spirits whom he delighted to collect round him at Skelton—familiarly known as "Crazy" Castle. The club of the " Demoniacs," of which Sterne makes mention in his letters, may have had nothing very diabolical about it except the name ; but, headed as it was by the suspected ex-comrade of Wilkes and his brother monks of Medmenham, and recruited by gay militaires like Colonels Hall and Lee, and "fast" parsons like the Rev. "Panty" Lascelles (mock godson of Pantagruel) it was certainly a society in which the Vicar of Sutton could not expect to enroll himself without offence. We may fairly suppose therefore that it was to his association with these somewhat too "jolly companions" that Sterne owed that disfavour among decorous country circles, of which he shows resentful consciousness in the earlier chapters of *Tristram Shandy.*

But before we finally cross the line which separates the life of the obscure country parson from the life of the

famous author, a word or two must be said of that piece
of writing which was alluded to a few pages back as the
only known exception to the generally "professional" character of all Sterne's compositions of the Pre-Shandian era.
This was a piece in the allegoric-satirical style, which,
though not very remarkable in itself, may not improbably
have helped to determine its author's thoughts in the
direction of more elaborate literary efforts. In the year
1758 a dispute had arisen between a certain Dr. Topham,
an ecclesiastical lawyer in large local practice, and Dr.
Fountayne, the then Dean of York. This dispute had
originated in an attempt on the part of the learned
civilian, who appears to have been a pluralist of an
exceptionally insatiable order, to obtain the reversion of
one of his numerous offices for his son, alleging a promise
made to him on that behalf by the Archbishop. This
promise, which had in fact been given, was legally
impossible of performance, and upon the failure of his
attempt the disappointed Topham turned upon the Dean,
and maintained that by *him* at any rate he had been
promised another place of the value of five guineas per
annum, and appropriately known as the "Commissaryship
of Pickering and Pocklington." This the Dean denied,
and thereupon Dr. Topham fired off a pamphlet setting
forth the circumstances of the alleged promise, and
protesting against the wrong inflicted upon him by its
non-performance. At this point Sterne came to Dr.
Fountayne's assistance with a sarcastic apologue entitled
the "History of a good warm Watchcoat," which had "hung
up many years in the parish vestry," and showing how
this garment had so excited the cupidity of Trim, the sexton,
that "nothing would serve him but he must take it home,
to have it converted into a warm under petticoat for his
wife and a jerkin for himself against the winter." The

symbolization of Dr. Topham's snug "patent place,"
which he wished to make hereditary, under the image of
the good warm watchcoat is of course plain enough ; and
there is some humour in the way in which the parson
(the Archbishop) discovers that his incautious assent to
Trim's request had been given *ultra vires.* Looking
through the parish register, at the request of a labourer
who wished to ascertain his age, the parson finds express
words of bequest leaving the watchcoat "for the sole use of
the sextons of the church for ever, to be worn by them
respectively on winterly cold nights," and at the moment
when he is exclaiming, "Just Heaven ! what an escape
have I had ! Give this for a petticoat to Trim's wife !" he
is interrupted by Trim himself entering the vestry with
"the coat actually ript and cut out" ready for conversion
into a petticoat for his wife.   And we get a foretaste of
the familiar Shandian impertinence in the remark which
follows, that "there are many good similes subsisting in
the world, but which I have neither time to recollect nor
look for, which would give you an idea of the parson's
astonishment at Trim's impudence."   The emoluments of
"Pickering and Pocklington" appear under the figure of a
"pair of black velvet plush breeches" which ultimately "got
into the possession of one Lorry Slim (Sterne himself, of
course), an unlucky wight by whom they are still worn : in
truth, as you will guess, they are very thin by this time."

The whole thing is the very slightest of "skits," and
the quarrel having been accommodated before it could be
published, it was not given to the world until after its
author's death.   But it is interesting as his first known
attempt in this line of composition, and the grasping
sexton deserves remembrance if only as having handed
down his name to a far more famous descendant.

CHAPTER IV.

HITHERTO we have had to construct our conception of
Sterne out of materials of more or less plausible conjecture. We are now at last approaching the region of
positive evidence, and henceforward, down almost to
the last scene of all, Sterne's doings will be chronicled,
and his character revealed, by one who happens, in this
case, to be the best of all possible biographers—the man
himself. Not that such records are by any means always
the most trustworthy of evidence. There are some men
whose real character is never more effectually concealed
than in their correspondence. But it is not so with Sterne.
The careless, slipshod letters which Mdme. de Medalle
"pitchforked" into the book-market, rather than edited,
are highly valuable as pieces of autobiography. They are
easy, naive, and natural, rich in simple self-disclosure in
almost every page, and if they have more to tell us about
the man than the writer, they are yet not wanting in
instructive hints as to Sterne's methods of composition and
his theories of art.

It was in the year 1759 that the Vicar of Sutton and
Prebendary of York, already, no doubt, a stone of
stumbling and a rock of offence to many worthy people in

the county, conceived the idea of astonishing and scan-
dalizing them still further after a new and original fashion.
His impulses to literary production were probably various,
and not all of them, or perhaps the strongest of them, of the
artistic order. The first and most urgent was, it may be suspected, the simplest and most common of all such motive
forces. Sterne, in all likelihood, was in want of money.
He was not, perhaps, under the actual instruction of that
magister artium whom the Roman satirist has celebrated ;
for he declared, indeed, afterwards, that " he wrote not to
be fed, but to be famous." But the context of the passage shows that he only meant to deny any absolute com-
pulsion to write for mere subsistence. Between this sort
of constraint and that gentler form of pressure which
arises from the wish to increase an income sufficient for
one's needs, but inadequate to one's desires, there is a considerable difference ; and to repudiate the one is not to
disclaim the other. It is, at any rate, certain that Sterne
engaged at one time of his life in a rather speculative
sort of farming, and we have it from himself in a passage
in one of his letters, which may be jest, but reads more like
earnest, that it was his losses in this business that first
turned his attention to literature.[1] His thoughts once set
in that direction, his peculiar choice of subject and method
of treatment are easily comprehensible. Pantagruelic
burlesque came to him, if not naturally, at any rate by
" second nature." He had a strong and sedulously cultivated taste for Rabelaisian humour ; his head was crammed

---

[1] "I was once such a puppy myself," he writes to a certain baronet
whom he is attempting to discourage from speculative farming of
this sort, " and had my labour for my pains and two hundred
pounds out of pocket. Curse on farming ! (I said). Let us see if
the pen will not succeed better than the spade."

with all sorts of out-of-the-way learning constantly tickling
his comic sense by its very uselessness ; he relished more
keenly than any man the solemn futilities of mediæval
doctors, and the pedantic indecencies of casuist fathers ;
and along with all these temptations to an enterprise of
the kind upon which he entered, he had been experiencing
a steady relaxation of deterrent restraints. He had fallen
out with his uncle some years since,[2] and the quarrel had
freed him from at least one influence making for clerical
propriety of behaviour. His incorrigible levities had probably lost him the countenance of most of his more serious
acquaintances ; his satirical humour had as probably gained
him personal enemies not a few, and it may be that he
had gradually contracted something of that "naughty-
boy" temper, as we may call it, for which the deliberate and
ostentatious repetition of offences has an inexplicable charm.
It seems clear, too, that, growth for growth with this
spirit of bravado, there had sprung up—in somewhat incongruous companionship, perhaps—a certain sense of wrong.
Along with the impulse to give an additional shock to
the prejudices he had already offended, Sterne felt
impelled to vindicate what he considered the genuine
moral worth underlying the indiscretions of the offender.
What, then, could better suit him than to compose a novel
in which he might give full play to his simious humour,
startle more hideously than ever his straiter-laced neighbours, defiantly defend his own character, and caricature

---

[2] He himself indeed makes a particular point of this in explain-
ing his literary venture. " Now for your desire," he writes to a
correspondent in 1759, "of knowing the reason of my turning
author ? why truly I am tired of employing my brains for other
people's advantage. 'Tis a foolish sacrifice I have made for some
years for an ungrateful person."—*Letters*, i. 82.

whatever eccentric figure in the society around him might offer the most tempting butt for ridicule?

All the world knows how far he ultimately advanced beyond the simplicity of the conception, and into what far higher regions of art its execution led him. But I find no convincing reason for believing that *Tristram Shandy* had at the outset any more seriously artistic purpose than this ; and much indirect evidence that this, in fact, it was.

The humorous figure of Mr. Shandy is, of course, the Cervantic centre of the whole ; and it was out of him and his crotchets that Sterne no doubt intended from the first to draw the materials of that often unsavoury fun which was to amuse the light-minded and scandalize the demure. But it can hardly escape notice that the two most elaborate portraits in Vol. I.—the admirable but very flatteringly idealized sketch of the author himself in Yorick, and the Gilrayesque caricature of Dr. Slop—are drawn with a distinctly polemical purpose, defensive in the former case and offensive in the latter. On the other hand, with the disappearance of Dr. Slop, caricature of living persons disappears also ; while after the famous description of Yorick's death-bed, we meet with no more attempts at self-vindication. It seems probable, therefore, that long before the first two volumes were completed Sterne had discovered the artistic possibilities of " My Uncle Toby" and " Corporal Trim," and had realized the full potentialities of humour contained in the contrast between the two brothers Shandy. The very work of sharpening and deepening the outlines of this humorous antithesis, while it made the crack-brained philosopher more and more of a burlesque unreality, continually added new touches of life and nature to the lineaments of the

simple-minded soldier; and it was by this curious and
half-accidental process that there came to be added to the
gallery of English fiction one of the most perfect and
delightful portraits that it possesses.

We know from internal evidence that *Tristram
Shandy* was begun in the early days of 1759; and the
first two volumes were probably completed by about the
middle of the year. "In the year 1760," writes Sterne,
"I went up to London to publish my two first volumes
of *Shandy*." And it is stated in a note to this passage,
as cited in Scott's memoir, that the first edition was
published "the year before" in York. There is, however, no direct proof that it was in the hands of the
public before the beginning of 1760, though it is possible
that the date of its publication may just have fallen
within the year. But, at all events, on the 1st of January,
1760, an advertisement in the *Public Advertiser* informed
the world that "this day" was "published, printed on
superfine writing-paper, &c., *The Life and Opinions of
Tristram Shandy*. York. Printed for and sold by John
Hinxham, Bookseller in Stonegate." The great London
publisher, Dodsley, to whom the book had been offered,
and who had declined the venture, figures in the
advertisement as the principal London bookseller from
whom it was to be obtained. It seems that only a few
copies were in the first instance sent up to the London
market; but they fell into good hands, for there is
evidence that *Tristram Shandy* had attracted the
notice of at least one competent critic in the capital
before the month of January was out. But though the
metropolitan success of the book was destined to be
delayed for still a month or two, in York it had already
created a *furore* in more senses than one. For, in fact,

and no wonder, it had in many quarters given the deepest offence. Its Rabelaisian licence of incident and allusion was calculated to offend the proprieties—the provincial proprieties especially—even in that free-spoken age ; and there was that in the book, moreover, which a provincial society may be counted on to abominate, with a keener if less disinterested abhorrence than any sins against decency. It contained, or was supposed to contain, a broadly ludicrous caricature of one well-known local physician ; and an allusion, brief indeed and covert, but highly scandalous, to a certain "droll foible" attributed to another personage of much wider celebrity in the scientific world. The victim in the latter case was no longer living; and this circumstance brought upon Sterne a remonstrance from a correspondent, to which he replied in a letter so characteristic in many respects as to be worth quoting. His correspondent was a Dr. * * * * *, (asterisks for which it is now impossible to substitute letters) ; and the burden of what seem to have been several communications in speech and writing on the subject was the maxim, "de mortuis nil nisi bonum." With such seriousness and severity had his correspondent dwelt upon this adage, that "at length," writes Sterne, "you have made me as serious and as severe as yourself ; but, that the humours you have stirred up might not work too potently within me, I have waited four days to cool myself before I could set pen to paper to answer you." And thus he sets forth the results of his four days' deliberation :—

"De mortuis nil nisi bonum." I declare I have considered the wisdom and foundation of it over and over again as dispassionately and charitably as a good Christian can, and after all I can find nothing in it, or make more of it than a nonsensical lullaby of some nurse, put into Latin by some pedant, to be chanted by some hypocrite to the end of the world for the consolation of departing lechers. 'Tis, I own, Latin, and I think that is all the weight it has, for, in plain English, 'tis a loose and futile position below a dispute. " You are not to speak anything of the dead but what is good." Why so ? Who says so ? Neither reason nor Scripture. Inspired authors have done otherwise, and reason and common sense tell me that, if the characters of past ages and men are to be drawn at all, they are to be drawn like themselves, that is, with their excellencies and their foibles ; and it as much a piece of justice to the world, and to virtue, too, to do the one as the other. The ruling passion, *et les égarements du cœur*, are the very things which mark and distinguish a man's character, in which I would as soon leave out a man's head as his hobby-horse. However, if, like the poor devil of a painter, we must conform to the pious canon, " de mortuis, &c.," which I own has a spice of piety in the *sound* of it, and be obliged to paint both our angels and our devils out of the same pot, I then infer that our Sydenhams and our Sangrados, our Lucretias and our Messalinas, our Somersets and our Bolingbrokes, are alike entitled to statues, and all the historians or satirists who have said otherwise since they departed this life, from Sallust to S——e, are guilty of the crimes you charge me with, " cowardice and injustice." But why cowardice ? " Because 'tis not courage to attack a dead man who can't defend himself." But why do you doctors attack such a one with your incision knife ? Oh ! for the good of the living. 'Tis my plea.

And, having given this humorous twist to his argument, he glides off into extenuatory matter. He had not even, he protests, made as much as a surgical incision into his victim (Dr. Richard Mead, the friend of Bentley and of Newton, and a physician and physiologist of high repute in his day) ; he had but just scratched him, and that scarce skin-deep. As to the " droll foible " of Dr. Mead,

which he had made merry with, "it was not first reported
(even to the few who can understand the hint) by me,
but known before by every chambermaid and footman
within the bills of mortality"—a somewhat daring
assertion, one would imagine, considering what the droll
foible was; and Dr. Mead, continues Sterne, great man
as he was, had, after all, not fared worse than "a man
of twice his wisdom,"—to wit Solomon, of whom the
same remark had been made, that "they were both great
men, and like all mortal men had each their ruling
passion."

The mixture of banter and sound reasoning in this
reply is, no doubt, very skilful. But unfortunately neither
the reasoning nor the banter happens to meet the case of
this particular defiance of the "De mortuis" maxim, and
as a serious defence against a serious charge (which was
what the occasion required) Sterne's answer is altogether
futile. For the plea of "the good of the living," upon
which, after all, the whole defence, considered seriously,
rests, was quite inapplicable as an excuse for the incri-
minated passage. The only living persons who could possibly be affected by it, for good or evil, were those
surviving friends of the dead man, to whom Sterne's
allusion to what he called Dr. Mead's "droll foible" was
calculated to cause the deepest pain and shame.

The other matter of offence to Sterne's Yorkshire
readers was of a much more elaborate kind. In the person
of Dr. Slop, the grotesque man-midwife, who was to have
assisted, but missed assisting at Tristram's entry into the
world, the good people of York were not slow to recognize
the physical peculiarities and professional antecedents of
Dr. Burton, the local accoucheur, whom Archdeacon
Sterne had arrested as a Jacobite. That the portrait was

faithful to anything but the external traits of the original,
or was intended to reproduce anything more than these,
Sterne afterwards denied; and we have certainly no
ground for thinking that Burton had invited ridicule on
any other than the somewhat unworthy ground of the
curious ugliness of his face and figure. It is most unlikely
that his success as a practitioner in a branch of the medical art in which imposture is the most easily detected,
could have been earned by mere quackery; and he seems,
moreover, to have been a man of learning in more kinds
than one. The probability is that the worst that could
be alleged against him was a tendency to scientific
pedantry in his published writings, which was pretty sure
to tickle the fancy of Mr. Sterne. Unscrupulously, however,
as he was caricatured, the sensation which appears to have
been excited in the county by the burlesque portrait could
hardly have been due to any strong public sympathy with
the involuntary sitter. Dr. Burton seems, as a suspected
Jacobite, to have been no special favourite with the Yorkshire squirearchy in general, but rather the reverse thereof.
Ucalegon, however, does not need to be popular to arouse
his neighbour's interest in his misfortunes; and the caricature of Burton was doubtless resented on the *proximus
ardet* principle by many who feared that their turn was
coming next.

To all the complaints and protests which reached him
on the subject, Sterne would in any case probably
have been indifferent; but he was soon to receive encouragement which would have more than repaid a man of
his temper for twice the number of rebukes. For London
cared nothing for Yorkshire susceptibilities and Yorkshire
fears. Provincial notables might be libelled, and their
friends might go in fear of similar treatment, but all that

was nothing to "the town," and *Tristram Shandy* had taken the town by storm. We gather from a passage in the letter above quoted that as early as January 30 the book had "gained the very favourable opinion" of Mr. Garrick, afterwards to become the author's intimate friend; and it is certain that by the time of Sterne's arrival in London, in March, 1760, *Tristram Shandy* had become the rage.

To say of this extraordinary work that it defies analysis would be the merest inadequacy of commonplace. It was meant to defy analysis; it is of the very essence of its scheme and purpose that it should do so; and the mere attempt to subject it systematically to any such process would argue an altogether mistaken conception of the author's intent. Its full "official" style and title is *The Life and Opinions of Tristram Shandy, Gent.*, and it is difficult to say which it contains the less about—the opinions of Tristram Shandy or the events of his life. As a matter of fact, its proper description would be "The Opinions of Tristram Shandy's Father, with Some Passages from the Life of his Uncle." Its claim to be regarded as a biography of its nominal hero is best illustrated by the fact that Tristram is not born till the third volume, and not breeched till the sixth; that it is not till the seventh that he begins to play any active part in the narrative, appearing then only as a completely colourless and unindividualized figure, a mere vehicle for the conveyance of Sterne's own Continental *impressions de voyage;* and that in the last two volumes, which are entirely taken up with the incident of his uncle's courtship, he disappears from the story altogether. It is to be presumed, perhaps, though not very confidently, that the reader would have seen more of him if the tale had been continued; but how much or how little is quite uncertain. The real hero of the book is at the outset Mr. Shandy, senior, who is, later on, succeeded in this place of dignity by my uncle Toby. It not only served Sterne's purpose to confine himself mainly to these two characters, as the best whereon to display his powers, but it was part of his studied eccentricity to do so. It was a "point" to give as little as possible about Tristram Shandy in a life of Tristram Shandy; just as it was a point to keep the reader waiting throughout the year 1760 for their hero to be so much as born. In the first volume, therefore, the author does literally everything but make the slightest progress with his story. Starting off abruptly with a mock physiologic disquisition upon the importance of a proper ordering of their mental states on the part of the intending progenitors of children, he philosophizes gravely on this theme for two or three chapters; and then wanders away into an account of the local midwife, upon whose sole services Mrs. Shandy, in opposition to her husband, was inclined to rely. From the midwife it is an easy transition to her patron and protector, the incumbent of the parish, and this, in its turn, suggests a long excursus on the character, habits, appearance, home, friends, enemies, and finally death, burial, and epitaph of the Rev. Mr. Yorick. Thence we return to Mr. and Mrs. Shandy, and are made acquainted, in absurdly minute detail, with an agreement entered into between them with reference to the place of sojourn to be selected for the lady's accouchement, the burlesque deed which records this compact being actually set out at full length. Thence, again, we are beckoned away by the jester to join him in elaborate and not very edifying ridicule of the Catholic doctrine of ante-natal baptism; and thence—but it would be useless to follow further the windings and doublings of this literary hare.

Yet, though the book as one thus summarizes it, may appear a mere farrago of digressions, it nevertheless, after its peculiar fashion, advances. Such definite purpose as underlies the tricks and grimaces of its author is by degrees accomplished ; and before we reach the end of the first volume, the highly humorous if extravagantly idealized figure of Mr. Shandy takes bodily shape and consistency before our eyes. It is a mistake, I think, of Sir Walter Scott's to regard the portrait of this eccentric philosopher as intended for a satire upon perverted and deranged erudition—as the study of a man "whom too much and too miscellaneous learning had brought within a step or two of madness." Sterne's conception seems to me a little more subtle and less commonplace than that. Mr. Shandy, I imagine, is designed to personify not "crack-brained learning" so much as "theory run mad." He is possessed by a sort of Demon of the Deductive, ever impelling him to push his premises to new conclusions without ever allowing him time to compare them with the facts. No doubt we are meant to regard him as a learned man ; but his son gives us to understand distinctly and very early in the book that his crotchets were by no means those of a weak receptive mind, overladen with more knowledge than it could digest, but rather those of an over-active intelligence, far more deeply and constantly concerned with its own processes than with the thoughts of others. Tristram, indeed, dwells pointedly on the fact that his father's dialectical skill was not the result of training, and that he owed nothing to the logic of the schools. " He was certainly," says his son, " irresistible both in his orations and disputations," but that was because " he was born an orator " (Θεοδίδακτος). Persuasion hung upon his lips, and the elements of logic

and rhetoric were so blended in him, and withal he had
so shrewd a guess at the weaknesses and passions of his
respondent that nature might have stood up and said,
"This man is eloquent. And yet," continues the filial
panegyric,—

He had never read Cicero nor ⸢Quintilian de Oratore, nor
Aristotle nor Longinus among the ancients, nor Vossius, nor
Skioppius, nor Ramus nor Farnaby among the moderns : and
what is more astonishing he had never in his whole life the least
light or spark of subtilty struck into his mind by one single
lecture upon Crackenthorpe or Burgersdicius or any Dutch commentator : he knew not so much as in what the difference of an
argument *ad ignorantiam* and an argument *ad hominem* con-
sisted; and when he went up along with me to enter my name
at Jesus College, in * * * *, it was a matter of just wonder
with my worthy tutor and two or three fellows of that learned
society that a man who knew not so much as the names of his
tools should be able to work after that fashion with them.

Surely we all know men of this kind, and the con-
sternation—comparable only to that of M. Jourdain under
the impromptu carte-and-tierce of his servant-maid—
which their sturdy if informal dialectic will often spread
among many kinds of "learned societies." But such men
are certainly not of the class which Scott supposed to
have been ridiculed in the character of Walter Shandy.

Among the crotchets of this born dialectician was a
theory as to the importance of Christian names in
determining the future behaviour and destiny of the
children to whom they are given; and whatever
admixture of jest there might have been in some of his
other fancies, in this his son affirms he was absolutely
serious. He solemnly maintained the opinion "that there
was a strange kind of magic bias which good or bad

names, as he called them, irresistibly impressed upon
our character and conduct." How many Cæsars and
Pompeys, he would say, by mere inspiration of their
names have been rendered worthy of them. And how
many, he would add, are there who might have done
exceeding well in the world had not their characters and
spirits been totally depressed and Nicodemus'd into
nothing? He was astonished at parents failing to perceive that "when once a vile name was wrongfully or
injudiciously given, 'twas not like a case of a man's
character, which when wronged might afterwards be
cleared; and possibly some time or other, if not in the
man's life, at least after his death, be somehow or other
set to rights with the world." This name-giving injury,
he would say, "could never be undone; nay, he doubted
whether an Act of Parliament could reach it; he knew, as
well as you, that the Legislature assumed a power over
surnames; but for very strong reasons, which he could
give, it had never yet adventured, he would say, to go a
step further."

With all this extravagance, however, there was combined an admirable affectation of sobriety. Mr. Shandy
would have us believe that he was no blind slave to his
theory. He was quite willing to admit the existence of
names, which could not affect the character either for
good or evil—Jack, Dick, and Tom, for instance; and
such the philosopher styled "neutral names," affirming of
them "without a satire, that there had been as many
knaves and fools at least as wise and good men since the
world began, who had indifferently borne them, so that
like equal forces acting against each other in contrary
directions, he thought they mutually destroyed each
others effects; for which reason he would often declare

he would not give a cherrystone to choose among them.
Bob, which was my brother's name, was another of these
neutral kinds of Christian names which operated very
little either way ; and as my father happened to be at
Epsom when it was given him, he would ofttimes thank
heaven it was no worse." Forewarned of this peculiarity
of Mr. Shandy's, the reader is, of course, prepared to hear
that of all the names in the universe the philosopher
had the most unconquerable aversion for Tristram, "the
lowest and most contemptible opinion of it of anything in
the world." He would break off in the midst of one of
his frequent disputes on the subject of names, and "in a
spirited epiphonema, or rather erotesis," demand of his
antagonist "whether he would take upon him to say he
had ever remembered, whether he had ever read, or whether
he had ever heard tell of a man called Tristram performing anything great or worth recording. No, he would
say. Tristram ! the thing is impossible." It only
remained that he should have published a book in defence
of the belief, and sure enough " in the year sixteen," two
years before the birth of his second son, " he was at the
pains of writing an express dissertation simply upon the
word Tristram, showing the world with great candour and
modesty the grounds of his great abhorrence to the name."
And with this idea Sterne continues to amuse himself at
intervals till the end of the chapter.

That he does not so persistently amuse the reader it is,
of course, scarcely necessary to say. The jest has not
substance enough—few of Sterne's jests have—to stand
the process of continual attrition to which he subjects
it. But the mere historic gravity with which the
various turns of this monomania are recorded—to say
nothing of the seldom failing charm of the easy gossiping

style—prevent the thing from ever becoming utterly
tiresome. On the whole, however, one begins to grow
impatient for more of the same sort as the three admirable
chapters on the Rev. Mr. Yorick, and are not sorry to get
to the opening of the second volume with its half-tender,
half-humorous, and wholly delightful account of Uncle
Toby's difficulties in describing the siege operations before
Namur, and of the happy chance by which these difficulties
made him ultimately the fortunate possessor of a "hobby."

Throughout this volume there are manifest signs of
Sterne's unceasing interest in his own creations, and of
his increasing consciousness of creative power. Captain
Toby Shandy is but just lightly sketched-in in the first
volume, while Corporal Trim has not made his appearance
on the scene at all ; but before the end of the second we
know both of them thoroughly within and without.
Indeed, one might almost say that in the first half-dozen
chapters which so excellently recount the origin of
the corporal's fortification scheme, and the wounded
officer's delighted acceptance of it, every trait in the
simple characters—alike yet so different in their simplicity—of master and of man becomes definitely fixed in
the reader's mind. And the total difference between the
second and the first volume in point of fulness, variety,
and colour is most marked. The artist, the inventor, the
master of dialogue, the comic dramatist in fact as
distinct from the humorous essayist, would almost seem
to have started into being as we pass from the one volume
to the other. There is nothing in the drolleries of the
first volume—in the broad jests upon Mr. Shandy's
crotchets, or even in the subtler humour of the intellectual
collision between these crotchets and his brother's plain
sense—to indicate the kind of power displayed in that

remarkable colloquy à *quatre*, which begins with the arrival of Dr. Slop and ends with Corporal Trim's recital of the Sermon on Conscience. Wit, humour, irony, quaint learning, shrewd judgment of men and things, of these Sterne had displayed abundance already ; but it is not in the earlier but in the later half of the first instalment of *Tristram Shandy* that we first become conscious that he is something more than the possessor of all these things : that he is gifted with the genius of creation and has sent forth new beings into that world of immortal shadows which to many of us is more real than our own.

CHAPTER V.

(1760—1762.)

STERNE alighted from the York mail just as Byron
"awoke one morning," to "find himself famous." Seldom
indeed has any lion so suddenly discovered been pursued
so eagerly and by such a distinguished crowd of hunters.
The chase was remarkable enough to have left a lasting
impression on the spectators; for it was several years
after (in 1773) that Dr. Johnson, by way of fortifying his
very just remark that "any man who has a name or who
has the power of pleasing will be generally invited in
London," observed gruffly that "the man Sterne," he was
told, "had had engagements for three months." And truly
it would appear from abundant evidence that "the man
Sterne" gained such a social triumph as might well have
turned a stronger head than his. Within twenty-four
hours after his arrival, his lodgings in Pall Mall were
besieged by a crowd of fashionable visitors; and in a few
weeks he had probably made the acquaintance of "everybody who was anybody" in the London society of that
day.

How thoroughly he relished the delights of celebrity is

revealed, with a simple vanity which almost disarms criticism, in many a passage of his correspondence. In one of his earliest letters to Miss Fourmantelle, we find him proudly relating to her how already he " was engaged to ten noblemen and men of fashion." Of Garrick, who had warmly welcomed the humourist whose merits he had been the first to discover, Sterne says that he had " promised him at dinner to numbers of great people." Among these great people who sought him out for themselves was that discerning patron of ability in every shape, Lord Rockingham. In one of the many letters which Madame de Medalle flung dateless upon the world, but which from internal evidence we can assign to the early months of 1760, Sterne writes that he is about to " set off with a grand retinue of Lord Rockingham's (in whose suite I move) for Windsor" to witness, it should seem, an installation of a Knight of the Garter. It is in his letters to Miss Fourmantelle, however, that his almost boyish exultation at his London triumph discloses itself most frankly. " My rooms," he writes, " are filling every hour with great people of the first rank, who strive who shall most honour me." Never, he believes, had such homage been rendered to any man by devotees so distinguished. "The honours paid me were the greatest that were ever known from the great."

The self-painted portrait is not, it must be confessed, altogether an attractive one. It is somewhat wanting in dignity, and its air of over-inflated complacency is at times slightly ridiculous. But we must not judge Sterne in this matter by too severe a standard. He was by nature neither a dignified nor a self-contained man : he had a head particularly unfitted to stand sudden elevation ; and it must be allowed that few men's power of resisting

giddiness at previously unexplored altitudes was ever so
severely tried.   It was not only "the great" in the sense
of the high in rank and social distinction by whom he
was courted ; he was welcomed also by the eminent in
genius and learning : and it would be no very difficult
task for him to flatter himself that it was the latter form
of recognition which he really valued most.   Much, at
any rate, in the way of undue elation may be forgiven to
a country clergyman who suddenly found himself the
centre of a court, which was regularly attended by
statesmen, wits, and leaders of fashion, and with which
even bishops condescended to open gracious diplomatic
communication.   "Even all the bishops," he writes,
"have sent their compliments ; " and though this can
hardly have been true of the whole episcopal bench,
it is certain that Sterne received something more than a
compliment from one bishop, who was a host in himself.
He was introduced by Garrick to Warburton, and received high encouragement from that formidable prelate.[1]

The year 1760, however, was to bring to Sterne more
solid gains than that of mere celebrity, or even than the
somewhat precarious money profits which depend on
literary vogue.   Only a few weeks after his arrival in
town he was presented by Lord Falconberg with the
curacy of Coxwold, " a sweet retirement," as he describes
it, " in comparison of Sutton,"—at which he was in future
to pass most of the time spent by him in Yorkshire.
What obtained him this piece of preferment is unknown.

---

[1] It is admitted, moreover, in the correspondence with Miss
Fourmantelle that Sterne received something more substantial
from the Bishop in the shape of a purse of gold ; and this strange
present gave rise to a scandal on which something will be said
hereafter.

It may be that *Tristram Shandy* drew the Yorkshire
peer's attention to the fact that there was a Yorkshireman
of genius living within a few miles of a then vacant
benefice in his lordship's gift ; and that this was enough
for him.   But Sterne himself says—in writing a year or
so afterwards to a lady of his acquaintance—" I hope I
have been of some service to his lordship, and he has
sufficiently requited me :" and in the face of this plain
assertion, confirmed as it is by the fact that Lord Falconberg was on terms of friendly intimacy with the Vicar
of Coxwold at a much later date than this, we may
dismiss idle tales about Sterne's having " black-mailed "
the patron out of a presentation to a benefice worth no
more, after all, than some 70*l*. a year net.

There is somewhat more substance, however, in the
scandal which got abroad with reference to a certain alleged
transaction between Sterne and Warburton.   Before Sterne
had been many days in London, and while yet his person
and doings were the natural subjects of the newest gossip,
a story found its way into currency to the effect that the
new-made Bishop of Gloucester had found it advisable to
protect himself against the satiric humour of the author
of the *Tristram Shandy* by a substantial present of
money.   Coming to Garrick's ears, it was repeated by
him—whether seriously or in jest—to Sterne, from whom
it evoked a curious letter which in Madame de Medalle's
collection has been studiously hidden away among the
correspondence of seven years later.   " 'Twas for all the
world," he began, " like a cut across my finger with a
sharp pen-knife.   I saw the blood—gave it a suck, wrapt
it up, and thought no more about it. . . . . The story
you told me of Tristram's pretended tutor this morning "—
(the scandal was, that Warburton had been threatened

with caricature in the next volume of the novel, under
the guise of the hero's tutor)—"this vile story, I say,
though I then saw both how and where it wounded, I
felt little from it at first, or, to speak more honestly
(though it ruins my simile), I felt a great deal of pain
from it, but affected an air, usual in such accidents, of
feeling less than I had." And he goes on to repudiate,
it will be observed, not so much the moral offence
of corruption, in receiving money to spare Warburton, as
the intellectual solecism of selecting him for ridicule.
"What the devil!" he exclaims, "is there no one
learned blockhead throughout the schools of misapplied
seience in the (Siristian world to make a tutor of for
my Tristram—are we so run out of stock that there is
no one lumber-headed, muddle-headed, mortar-headed,
pudding-head chap among our doctors ? . . . . but I must
disable my judgment by choosing a Warburton." Later
on, in a letter to his friend, Mr. Croft, at Stillington,
whom the scandal had reached through a " society journal "
of the time, he asks whether people would suppose he
would be " such a fool as to fall foul of Dr. Warburton,
my best friend, by representing him so weak a man ; or
by telling such a lie of him as his giving me a purse to
buy off the tutorship of Tristram—or that I should be
fool enough to own that I had taken a purse for that
purpose." It will be remarked that Sterne does not here
deny having received a purse from Warburton, but only
his having received it by way of black-mail : and the most
mysterious part of the affair is that Sterne did actually
receive the strange present of a "purse of gold " from
Warburton (whom at that time he did not know nor had
ever seen) ; and that he admits as much in one of his
letters to Miss Fourmantelle. " I had a purse of guineas

given me yesterday by a bishop," he writes triumphantly, but without volunteering any explanation of this extra-ordinary gift. Sterne's letter to Garrick was forwarded, it would seem, to Warburton ; and the Bishop thanks Garrick for having procured for him "the confutation of an impertinent story the first moment I heard of it." This, however, can hardly count for much. If Warburton had really wished Sterne to abstain from caricaturing him, he would be as anxious—and for much the same reasons—to conceal the fact as to suppress the caricature. He would naturally have the disclosure of it reported to Sterne for formal contradiction, as in fulfilment of a virtual term in the bargain between them. The epithet of "irre-vocable scoundrel" which he afterwards applied to Sterne, is of less importance, as proceeding from War-burton, than it would have been had it come from any one not habitually employing Warburton's peculiar vocabulary ; but it at least argues no very cordial feeling on the Bishop's side. And, on the whole, one regrets to feel, as I must honestly confess that I do feel, far less con-fident of the groundlessness of this rather unpleasant story than could be wished. It is impossible to forget, how-ever, that while the ethics of this matter were undoubtedly less strict in those days than they are—or, at any rate, are recognized as being—in our own, there is nothing in Sterne's character to make us suppose him to have been at all in advance of the morality of his time.

The incumbent-designate did not go down at once to take possession of his temporalities. His London triumph had not yet run its course. The first edition of Vols. I. and II. of *Tristram Shandy* was exhausted in some three months. In April, Dodsley brought out a second ; and, concurrently with the advertisement of its issue, there appeared—in somewhat incongruous companionship—the announcement, " Speedily will be published, The Sermons of Mr. Yorick." The judicious Dodsley, or possibly the judicious Sterne himself (acute enough in matters of this kind) had perceived that now was the time to publish a series of sermons by the very unclerical lion of the day. There would—they no doubt thought—be an undeniable piquancy, a distinct flavour of semi-scandalous incongruity in listening to the Word of Life from the lips of this loose-tongued droll ; and the more staid and serious the sermon, the more effective the contrast. There need not have been much trouble in finding the kind of article required : and we may be tolerably sure that, even if Sterne did not perceive that fact for himself, his publisher hastened to inform him that " anything would do." Two of his pulpit discourses, the Assize Sermon and the Charity Sermon, had already been thought worthy of publication by their author in a separate form ; and the latter of these found a place in the series ; while the rest seem to have been simply the chance sweepings of the parson's sermon-drawer. The critics who find wit, eccentricity, flashes of Shandyism, and what not else of the same sort in these discourses, must be able—or so it seems to me—to discover these phenomena anywhere. To the best of my own judgment, the Sermons are—with but few and partial exceptions—of the most commonplace character; platitudinous with the platitudes of a thousand pulpits, and insipid with the *crambe repetita* of a hundred thousand homilies. A single extract will fully suffice for a specimen of Sterne's pre-Shandian homiletic style ; his post-Shandian manner was very different, as we shall see. The preacher is discoursing upon the well-worn subject of the inconsistencies of human character :—

If such a contrast was only observable in the different stages
of a man's life, it would cease to be either a matter of wonder
or of just reproach.　Age, experience, and much reflection may
naturally enough be supposed to alter a man's sense of things,
and so entirely to transform him that, not only in outward
appearance but in the very cast and turn of his mind, he may
be as unlike and different from the man he was twenty or thirty
years ago as he ever was from anything of his own species.
This, I say, is naturally to be accounted for, and in some cases
might be praiseworthy too; but the observation is to be made
of men in the same period of their lives that in the same day,
sometimes on the very same action, they are utterly inconsistent
and irreconcilable with themselves.　Look at the man in one
light and he shall seem wise, penetrating, discreet, and brave:
behold him in another point of view, and you see a creature all
over folly and indiscretion, weak and timorous as cowardice
and indiscretion can make him.　A man shall appear gentle,
courteous, and benevolent to all mankind; follow him into his
own house, maybe you see a tyrant morose and savage to all
whose happiness depends upon his kindness.　A third, in his
general behaviour, is found to be generous, disinterested,
humane, and friendly.　Hear but the sad story of the friendless
orphans too credulously trusting all their whole substance into
his hands, and he shall appear more sordid, more pitiless and
unjust than the injured themselve have bitterness to paint him.
Another shall be charitable to the poor, uncharitable in his cen-
sures and opinions of all the rest of the world besides: temperate
in his appetites, intemperate in his tongue; shall have too much
conscience and religion to cheat the man who trusts him, and
perhaps as far as the business of debtor and creditor extends
shall be just and scrupulous to the uttermost mite; yet in
matters of full or great concern, where he is to have the handling
of the party's reputation and good name, the dearest, the tenderest property the man has, he will do him irreparable damage,
and rob him there without measure or pity.—Sermon XI.—*On
Evil Speaking.*

There is clearly nothing particularly striking in all

that, even conveyed as it is in Sterne's effective, if loose
and careless, style ; and it is no unfair sample of the
whole. The calculation, however, of the author and his
shrewd publisher was that, whatever the intrinsic merits
or demerits of these sermons, they would "take" on
the strength of the author's name; nor, it would seem,
was their calculation disappointed. The edition of this
series of sermons now lying before me is numbered the
sixth, and its date is 1764; which represents a demand
for a new edition every nine months or so, over a space
of four years. They may, perhaps, have succeeded, too,
in partially reconciling a certain serious-minded portion
of the public to the author. Sterne evidently hoped
that they might; for we find him sending a copy to
Warburton, in the month of June, immediately after the
publication of the book. and receiving in return a letter
of courteous thanks, and full of excellent advice as to
the expediency of avoiding scandal by too hazardous a
style of writing in future. Sterne, in reply, protests
that he would "willingly give no offence to mortal by
anything which could look like the least violation of
either decency or good manners;" but—and it is an
important "but"—he cannot promise to "mutilate everything" in *Tristram* "down to the prudish humour of
every particular" (individual), though he will do his best;
but, in any case, "laugh, my Lord, I will, and as loudly
as I can." And laugh he did, and in such Rabelaisian
fashion that the Bishop (somewhat inconsistently for a
critic who had welcomed Sterne on the appearance of the
first two volumes expressly as the "English Rabelais")
remarked of him afterwards with characteristic vigour
in a letter to a friend that he fears the fellow is an
"irrevocable scoundrel."

The volumes, however, which earned "the fellow" this Episcopal benediction were not given to the world till the next year. At the end of May or beginning of June, 1760, Sterne went to his new home at Coxwold, and his letters soon begin to show him to us at work upon further records of Mr. Shandy's philosophical theory-spinning and the simpler pursuits of his excellent brother. It is probable that this year, 1760, was on the whole the happiest year of Sterne's life. His health, though always feeble, had not yet finally given way ; and though the " vile cough " which was to bring him more than once to death's door, and at last to force it open, was already troubling him, he had that within him which made it easy to bear up against all such physical ills. His spirits, in fact, were at their highest. His worldly affairs were going at least as smoothly as they ever went. He was basking in that sunshine of fame which was so delightful to a temperament differing from that of the average Englishman, as does the physique of the Southern races from that of the hardier children of the North ; and lastly, he was exulting in a new-born sense of creative power which no doubt made the composition of the earlier volumes of *Tristram* a veritable labour of love.

But the witty division of literary spinners into silk-worms and spiders—those who spin because they are full, and those who do so because they are empty—is not exhaustive. There are human silk-worms who become gradually transformed into spiders—men who begin writing in order to unburden a full imagination, and who, long after that process has been completely performed, continue writing in order to fill an empty belly ; and though Sterne did not live long enough to "write himself out," there are certain indications that he would not have

left off writing if and when he felt that this stage of
exhaustion had arrived.   His artistic impulses were
curiously combined with a distinct admixture of the
"pot-boiler" spirit; and it was with something of the
complacency of an annuitant that he looked forward to
giving the public a couple of volumes of *Tristram
Shandy* every year as long as they would stand it.   In
these early days, however, there was no necessity even to
discuss the probable period either of the writer's inspiration or of the reader's appetite.   At present, the public
were as eager to consume more Shandyism as Sterne was
ready to produce it: the demand was as active as the
supply was easy.   By the end of the year Vols. III. and
IV. were in the press, and on January 27, 1761, they
made their appearance.   They had been disposed of in
advance to Dodsley for 380*l*.—no bad terms of remu-
neration in those days; but it is still likely enough that
the publisher made a profitable bargain.   The new volumes
sold freely, and the public laughed at them as heartily as
their two predecessors.   Their author's vogue in London,
whither he went in December, 1760, to superintend publication, was as great during the next spring as it had
been in the last.   The tide of visitors again set in in all
its former force and volume towards the "genteel lodgings."   His dinner list was once more full, and he was
feasted and flattered by wits, beaux, courtiers, politicians,
and titled-lady lion-hunters as sedulously as ever.   His
letters, especially those to his friends the Crofts, of
Stillington, abound, as before, in touches of the same
amusing vanity.   With how delicious a sense of self-
importance must he have written these words, "You made
me and my friends very merry with the accounts current
at York of my being forbad the Court, but they do not

consider what a considerable person they make of me
when they suppose either my going or not going there
is a point that ever enters the K.'s head; and for those
about him, I have the honour either to stand so personally well-known to them, or to be so well represented by those of the first rank as to fear no accident
of the kind." Amusing, too, is it to note the familiarity,
as of an old *habitué* of Ministerial antechambers, with
which this country parson discusses the political changes
of that interesting year; though scarcely more amusing perhaps than the solemnity with which his daughter disguises
the identity of the new Premier under the title B——e;
and by a similar use of initials attempts to conceal the
momentous state secret that the D. of R. had been removed
from the place of Groom of the Chambers, and that Sir F.
D. had succeeded T. as Chancellor of the Exchequer.
Occasionally, however, the interest of his letters changes
from personal to public, and we get a glimpse of scenes
and personages that have become historical. He was
present in the House of Commons at the first grand
debate on the German war after the Great Commoner's
retirement from office—"the pitched battle," as Sterne
calls it, "wherein Mr. P. was to have entered and thrown
down the gauntlet" in defence of his military policy.
Thus he describes it :—

There never was so full a house—the gallery full to the top
—I was there all the day; when lo! a political fit of the gout
seized the great combatant—he entered not the lists. Beckford
got up and begged the House, as he saw not his right honourable
friend there, to put off the debate—it could not be done: so
Beckford rose up and made a most long, passionate, incoherent
speech in defence of the German war, but very severe upon the
unfrugal manner it was carried on, in which he addressed him.

self principally to the C[hancellor] of the E[xchequer], and laid
him on terribly. . . . . Legge answered Beckford very rationally
and coolly. Lord N. spoke long. Sir F. D[ashwood] maintained the German war was most pernicious. . . . . Lord
B[arrington] at last got up and spoke half an hour with great
plainness and temper, explained many hidden things relating to
these accounts in favour of the late K., and told two or three
conversations which had passed between the K. and himself
relative to these expenses, which cast great honour upon the K.'s
character. This was with regard to the money the K. had
secretly furnished out of his own pocket to lessen the account
of the Hanover-score brought us to discharge. Beckford and
Barrington abused all who fought for peace and joined in the
cry for it, and Beckford added that the reasons of wishing a peace
now were the same as at the peace of Utrecht—that the people
behind the curtain could not both maintain the war and their
places too, so were for making another sacrifice of the nation to
their own interests. After all, the cry for a peace is so general
that it will certainly end in one.

And then the letter, recurring to personal matters
towards the close, records the success of Vols. III. and
IV. " One half of the town abuse my book as bitterly as
the other half cry it up to the skies—the best is they
abuse and buy it, and at such a rate that we are going
on with a second edition as fast as possible." This was
written only in the first week of March, so that the
edition must have been exhausted in little more than a
month. It was, indeed, another triumph; and all through
this spring up to midsummer did Sterne remain in London to enjoy it. But with three distinct flocks awaiting
a renewal of his pastoral ministrations in Yorkshire it
would scarcely have done for him, even in those easy-going
days of the Establishment, to take up his permanent abode
at the capital; and early in July he returned to Coxwold.

From the middle of this year, 1761, the scene begins
to darken, and from the beginning of the next year
onward Sterne's life was little better than a truceless
struggle with the disease to which he was destined, prematurely, to succumb. The wretched constitution, which
in common with his short-lived brothers and sisters, he had
inherited probably from his father, already began to show
signs of breaking up. Invalid from the first, it had doubtless been weakened by the hardships of Sterne's early years,
and yet further, perhaps, by the excitements and dissipa-
tions of his London life ; nor was the change from the
gaieties of the capital to hard literary labour in a country
parsonage calculated to benefit him as much as it might
others. Shandy Hall, as he christened his pretty
parsonage at Coxwold, and as the house, still standing, is
called to this day, soon became irksome to him. The
very reaction begotten of unwonted quietude acted on
his temperament with a dispiriting rather than a soothing
effect. The change from his full and stimulating life in
London to the dull round of clerical duties in a Yorkshire
village, might well have been depressing to a mind better
balanced and ballasted than his. To him, with his light
pleasure-loving nature, it was as the return of the school-
boy from pantomimes and pony-riding to the more sober
delights of Dr. Swishtail's ; and, in a letter to Hall
Stevenson, Sterne reveals his feelings with all the juvenile
frankness of one of the doctor's pupils.

I rejoice you are in London, rest you there in peace ; here 'tis
the devil. You was a good prophet. I wish myself back again,
as you told me I should, but not because a thin, death-doing,
pestiferous north-east wind blows in a line directly from Crazy
Castle turret fresh upon me in this cuckoldly retreat (for I
value the north-east wind and all its powers not a straw), but

the transition from rapid motion to absolute rest was too violent.
I should have walked about the streets of York ten days, as a
proper medium to have passed through before I entered upon
my rest; I stayed but a moment, and I have been here but a few,
to satisfy me. I have not managed my miseries like a wise
man, and if God for my consolation had not poured forth the
spirit of Shandyism unto me, which will not suffer me to
think two moments upon any grave subject, I would else just
now lay down and die.

It is true, he adds, in the next sentence, that in half
an hour's time " I'll lay a guinea I shall be as merry as a
monkey, and forget it all," but such sudden revulsions of
high spirits can hardly be allowed to count for much
against the prevailing tone of discontented *ennui* which
pervades this letter.

Apart moreover from Sterne's regrets of London, his
country home was becoming from other causes a less
pleasant place of abode. His relations with his wife were
getting less and less cordial every year. With a perversity
sometimes noticeable in the wives of distinguished men,
Mrs. Sterne had failed to accept with enthusiasm the *rôle*
of distant and humbly admiring spectator of her brilliant
husband's triumphs. Accept it of course she did, being
unable, indeed, to help herself ; but it is clear that when
Sterne returned home after one of his six months' revels
in the gaieties of London, his wife, who had been vege-
tating the while in the retirement of Yorkshire, was not
in the habit of welcoming him with effusion. Perceiving
so clearly that her husband preferred the world's society
to hers, she naturally, perhaps, refused to disguise her
preference of her own society to his. Their estrangement,
in short, had grown apace, and had already brought them
to that stage of mutual indifference which is at once so

comfortable and so hopeless—secure alike against the risk
of "scenes" and the hope of reconciliation, shut fast in
its exemption from *amantium iræ* against all possibility
of *redintegratio amoris*. To such perfection indeed had
the feeling been cultivated on both sides, that Sterne in
the letter above quoted can write of his conjugal relations
in this philosophic strain :—

As to matrimony I should be a beast to rail at it, for my wife
is easy, but the world is not, and had I stayed from her a second
longer it would have been a burning shame—else she declares
herself happier without me.   But not in anger is this declara-
ration made [the most fatal point, of course, about it], but in
pure, sober, good sense, built on sound experience.   She hopes
you will be able to strike a bargain for me before this twelve-
month to lead a bear round Europe, and from this hope from
you I verily believe it is that you are so high in her favour at
present. She swears you are a fellow of wit, though humorous ; [2]
a funny, jolly soul, though somewhat splenetic, and (bating
the love of women) as honest as gold.   How do you like the
simile ?

There is, perhaps, a touch of affected cynicism in the
suggestion that Mrs. Sterne's liking for one of her
husband's friends was wholly based upon the expecta-
tion that he would rid her of her husband ; but mutual
indifference must, it is clear, have reached a pretty
advanced stage before such a remark could, even half in
jest, be possible.   And with one more longing lingering
look at the scenes which he had quitted for a lot like that

---

[2] It is curious to note as a point in the chronology of language
how exclusive is Sterne's employment of the words "humour,"
"humourist," in their older sense of "whimsicality," "an eccentric." The later change in its meaning gives to the word "though"
in the above passage an almost comic effect.

of the Duke of Buckingham's dog, upon whom his master pronounced the maledictory wish that "he were married and lived in the country," this characteristic letter concludes :—

Oh, Lord! now are you going to Ranelagh to-night, and I am sitting sorrowful as the prophet was when the voice cried out to him and said, "What do'st thou here, Elijah?" 'Tis well that the spirit does not make the same at Coxwold, for unless for the few sheep left me to take care of in the wilderness, I might as well, nay better, be at Mecca. When we find we can, by a shifting of places, run away from ourselves, what think you of a jaunt there before we finally pay a visit to the Vale of Jehoshaphat. As ill a fame as we have, I trust I shall one day or other see you face to face, so tell the two colonels if they love good company to live righteously and soberly *as you do*, and then they will have no doubts or dangers within or without them. Present my best and warmest wishes to them, and advise the eldest to prop up his spirits, and get a rich dowager before the conclusion of the peace. Why will not the advice suit both, *par nobile fratrum?*

In conclusion, he tells his friend that the next morning, if Heaven permit, he begins the fifth volume of *Shandy*, and adds defiantly that he "cares not a curse for the critics," but "will load my vehicle with what goods He sends me, and they may take 'em off my hands or let 'em alone."

The allusions to foreign travel in this letter were made with something more than a jesting intent. Sterne had already begun to be seriously alarmed, and not without reason, about the condition of his health. He shrank from facing another English winter, and meditated a southward flight so soon as he should have finished his fifth and sixth volumes, and seen them safe in the printer's

hands. His publisher he had changed, for what reason is
not known, and the firm of Becket and De Hondt had
taken the place of Dodsley. Sterne hoped by the end
of the year to be free to depart from England, and already
he had made all arrangements with his ecclesiastical
superiors for the necessary leave of absence. He seems to
have been treated with all consideration in the matter.
His archbishop, on being applied to, at once excused him
from parochial work for a year, and promised, if it
should be necessary, to double that term. Fortified with
this permission, Sterne bade farewell to his wife and
daughter, and betook himself to London with his now
completed volumes, at the setting in of the winter. On
the 21st of December they made their appearance, and in
about three weeks from that date their author left England
with the intention of wintering in the South of France.
There were difficulties, however, of more kinds than one
which had first to be faced—a pecuniary difficulty which
Garrick met by a loan of 20*l.*, and a political difficulty for
the removal of which Sterne had to employ the good
offices of new acquaintance later on. He reached Paris
about the 17th of January, 1762, and there met with a
reception which interposed, as might have been expected,
the most effectual of obstacles to his further progress
southward. He was received in Paris with open arms,
and stepped at once within the charmed circle of the
philosophic salons. Again was the old intoxicating cup
presented to his lips—this time, too, with more dexterous
than English hands—and again did he drink deeply of it.
"My head is turned," he writes to Garrick, " with what
I see, and the unexpected honour I have met with here.
Tristram was almost as much known here as in London,
at least among your men of condition and learning, and

has got me introduced into so many circles ('tis comme à
Londres) I have just now a fortnight's dinners and
suppers on my hands." We may venture to doubt
whether French politeness had not been in one respect
taken somewhat too seriously by the flattered Englishman,
and whether it was much more than the name and general
reputation of *Tristram*, which was " almost as much
known " in Paris as in London. The dinners and suppers,
however, were at any rate no figures of speech, but very
liberal entertainments, at which Sterne appears to have
disported himself with all his usual unclerical *abandon*.
" I Shandy it away," he writes in his boyish fashion to
Garrick, "fifty times more than I was ever wont, talk
more nonsense than ever you heard me talk in all your
days, and to all sorts of people. ' Qui le diable est cet
homme-là ? ' said Choiseul, t'other day, ' ce Chevalier
Shandy ? ' " [We might be listening to one of Thackeray's
Irish heroes.] " You'll think me as vain as a devil was I
to tell you the rest of the dialogue." But there were distinguished Frenchmen who were ready to render to the
English author more important services than that of
offering him hospitality and flattery. Peace had not been
formally concluded between France and England, and the
passport with which Sterne had been graciously furnished
by Pitt was not of force enough to dispense him from
making special application to the French Government for
permission to remain in the country. In this request he
was influentially backed. " My application," he writes,
" to the Count de Choiseul goes on swimmingly, for not
only M. Pelletière (who by-the-bye sends ten thousand
civilities to you and Mrs. G.) has undertaken my affair,
but the Count de Limbourg. The Baron d'Holbach has
offered any security for the inoffensiveness of my behaviour

in France—'tis more, you rogue ! than you will do." And
then the orthodox, or professedly orthodox English divine,
goes on to describe the character and habits of his strange
new friend. "This Baron is one of the most learned
noblemen here, the great protector of wits and of the savans
who are no wits, keeps open house three days a week—his
house is now as yours was to me, my own—he lives at great
expense." Equally communicative is he as to his other great
acquaintances. Among these were the Count de Bissie, whom
by an "odd incident" (as it seemed to his unsuspecting
vanity) "I found reading *Tristram* when I was introduced to him, which I was," he adds (without perceiving
the connexion between this fact and the "incident"), "at
his desire ;" Mr. Fox and Mr. Macartney (afterwards
the Lord Macartney of Chinese celebrity) ; and the
Duke of Orleans (not yet Égalité) himself, "who has
suffered my portrait to be added to the number of some
odd men in his collection, and has had it taken most
expressively at full length by a gentleman who lives with
him." Nor was it only in the delights of society that
Sterne was now revelling. He was passionately fond of
the theatre, and his letters to Garrick are full of eager
criticism of the great French performers, intermingled
with flatteries, sometimes rather full-bodied than delicate,
of their famous English rival. Of Clairon, in *Iphigénie*, he
says "she is extremely great. Would to God you had one
or two like her. What a luxury to see you with one of such
power in the same interesting scene ! but 'tis too much."
Again he writes : "The French comedy I seldom visit ;
they act scarce anything but tragedies ; and the Clairon is
great, and Mdlle. Dumesmil in some parts still greater
than her. Yet I cannot bear preaching—I fancy I got a
surfeit of it in my younger days." And in a later letter :

After a vile suspension of three weeks, we are beginning
with our comedies and operas. Yours I hear never flourished
more ; here the comic actors were never so low, the tragedians
held up their heads in all senses. I have known *one little man*
support the theatrical world like a David Atlas upon his
shoulders, but Préville can't do half as much here, though Mad.
Clairon stands by him and sets her back to his. She is very
great, however, and highly improved since you saw her. She
also supports her dignity at table, and has her public day
every Thursday, when she gives to eat (as they say here) to all
that are hungry and dry. You are much talked of here, and
much expected, as soon as the peace will let you. These two
last days you have happened to engross the whole conversation
at the great houses where I was at dinner. 'Tis the greatest
problem in nature in this meridian that one and the same man
should possess such tragic and comic powers, and in such an
equilibrio as to divide the world for which of the two nature
intended him.

And while on this subject of the stage, let us pause for
a moment to glance at an incident which connects Sterne
with one of the most famous of his French contemporaries :—He has been asked " by a lady of talent "—he
tells Garrick, " to read a tragedy, and conjecture if it would
do for you ? 'Tis from the plan of Diderot ; and possibly
half a translation of it : *The Natural Son, or the Triumph of Virtue*, in five Acts. It has too much sentiment
in it (at least for me) ; the speeches too long, and savour
too much of preaching. This may be a second reason,
it is not to my taste—'tis all love, love, love, throughout,
without much separation in the characters. So I fear it
would not do for your stage, and perhaps for the very
reason which recommends it to a French one." It is
curious to see the " adaptator cerebrosuga " at work in
those days as in these ; though not, in this instance, as it

seems, with as successful results. *The Natural Son, or the Triumph of Virtue,* is not known to have reached either English readers or English theatrical audiences. The French original, as we know, fared scarcely better. "It was not until 1771," says Diderot's latest English biographer, "that the directors of the French Comedy could be induced to place *Le Fils Naturel* on the stage. The actors detested their task, and, as we can well believe, went sulkily through parts, which they had not taken the trouble to master. The public felt as little interest in the piece as the actors had done, and after one or two representations, it was put aside."[3]

Another, and it is to be guessed a too congenial acquaintance, formed by Sterne in Paris, was that of Crébillon ; and with him he concluded " a convention," unedifying enough whether in jest or earnest : " As soon as I get to Toulouse he has agreed to write me an expostulatory letter upon the indecorums of *T. Shandy,* which is to be answered by recrimination upon the liberties in his own works. These are to be printed together, Crébillon against Sterne, Sterne against Crébillon, —the copy to be sold, and the money equally divided. This is good Swiss-policy," he adds ; and the idea (which was never carried out) had certainly the merit of ingenuity, if no other.

The words " as soon as I get to Toulouse," in a letter written from Paris on the 10th of April, might well have reminded Sterne of the strange way in which he had carried out his intention of " wintering in the south." He insists, however, upon the curative effects of his winter of gaiety in Paris. " I am recovered greatly," he says ; " and

---

[3] Morley : " Diderot and the Encyclopædists," ii. 305.

if I could spend one whole winter at Toulouse, I should be
fortified in my inner man beyond all danger of relapsing."
There was another too for whom this change of climate
had become imperatively necessary. For three winters
past his daughter Lydia, now fourteen years old, had
been suffering severely from asthma, and needed to try
"the last remedy of a warmer and softer air." Her father
therefore was about to solicit passports for his wife and
daughter, with a view to their joining him at once in Paris,
whence, after a month's stay, they were to depart together
for the south. This application for passports he intended,
he said, to make "this week:" and it would seem that
the intention was carried out: but, for reasons explained
in a letter which Mr. Fitzgerald was the first to publish,
it was not till the middle of the next month that he was
able to make preparation for their joining him. From this
letter—written to his Archbishop, to request an extension
of his leave—we learn that while applying for the passports he was attacked with a fever, "which has ended
the worst way it could for me, in a défluxion (de) poitrine,
as the French physicians call it. It is generally fatal to
weak lungs, so that I have lost in ten days all I have
gained since I came here: and from a relaxation of my
lungs have lost my voice entirely, that 'twill be much if
I ever quite recover it. This evil sends me directly to
Toulouse, for which I set out from this place directly
my family arrives." Evidently there was no time to
be lost, and a week after the date of this letter we find
him in communication with Mrs. and Miss Sterne, and
making arrangements for what was, in those days, a somewhat formidable undertaking—the journey of two ladies
from the north of England to the centre of France. The
correspondence which ensued may be said to give us the

last pleasant glimpse of Sterne's relations with his wife.
One can hardly help suspecting, of course, that it was his
solicitude for the safety and comfort of his much-loved
daughter that mainly inspired the affectionate anxiety
which pervades these letters to Mrs. Sterne ; but their
writer is, at the very least, entitled to credit for allowing
no difference of tone to reveal itself in the terms in which
he speaks of wife and child.   And whichever of the two
he was mainly thinking of, there is something very en-
gaging in the thoughtful minuteness of his instructions to
the two women travellers, the earnestness of his attempts
to inspire them with courage for their enterprise, and the
sincere fervour of his many commendations of them to
the Divine keeping.   The mixture of "canny" counsel
and pious invocation has frequently a droll effect : as
when the advice to " give the custom-house officers what I
told you, and at Calais more, if you have much Scotch
snuff ;" and " to drink small Rhenish to keep you cool,
that is if you like it," is rounded off by the ejaculation
" So God in Heaven prosper and go along with you ! "
Letter after letter did he send them, full of such re-
minders as that "they have bad pins and vile needles
here," that it would be advisable to bring with them a
strong bottle-screw, and a good stout copper-teakettle ;
till at last, in the final words of preparation, his language
assumes something of the solemnity of a general addressing
his army on the eve of a well-nigh desperate enterprise :
" Pluck up your spirits,—trust in God, in me, and your-
selves ; with this, was you put to it, you would en-
counter all these difficulties ten times told.   Write
instantly, and tell me you triumph over all fears—tell
me Lydia is better, and a help-mate to you. You say
she grows like me : let her show me she does so in her

contempt of small dangers, and fighting against the apprehensions of them, which is better still."

At last this anxiously awaited journey was taken ; and,
on Thursday, July 7, Mrs. Sterne and her daughter
arrived in Paris. Their stay there was not long—not
much extended, probably, beyond the proposed week.
For Sterne's health had, some ten days before the arrival'
of his family, again given him warning to depart quickly.
He had but a few weeks recovered from the fever of
which he spoke in his letter to the Archbishop, when
he again broke a blood-vessel in his lungs. It happened
in the night, and "finding in the morning that I was
likely to bleed to death, I sent immediately," he says, in a
sentence which quaintly brings out the paradox of contemporary medical treatment, " for a surgeon to bleed me
at both arms. This saved me,"—i.e. did not kill me,—
" and, with lying speechless three days, I recovered upon
my back in bed : the breach healed, and in a week after
I got out." But the weakness which ensued, and the
subsequent " hurrying about," no doubt as cicerone of
Parisian sights to his wife and daughter, "made me think
it high time to haste to Toulouse." Accordingly, about
the 20th of the month, and "in the midst of such heats
that the oldest Frenchman never remembers the like,"
the party set off by way of Lyons and Montpellier for
their Pyrenean destination. Their journey seems to have
been a journey of many mischances, extraordinary discomfort, and incredible length : and it is not till the
second week in August that we again take up the broken
thread of his correspondence. Writing to Mr. Foley, his
banker in Paris, on the 14th of that month, he speaks of
its having taken him three weeks to reach Toulouse ; and
adds, that " in our journey we suffered so much from the

heats, it gives me pain to remember it. I never saw a
cloud from Paris to Nismes half as broad as a twenty-four sols
piece. Good God, we were toasted, roasted, grilled, stewed,
carbonaded, on one side or other, all the way : and being
all done through (*assez cuits*) in the day, we were eat up
at night by bugs and other unswept-out vermin, the legal
inhabitants, if length of possession give right, at every
inn on the way." A few miles from Beaucaire he broke
a hind wheel of his carriage, and was obliged in consequence " to sit five hours on a gravelly road without
one drop of water, or possibility of getting any ;" and
here, to mend the matter, he was cursed with " two
dough-hearted fools" for postilions, who "fell a-crying
' nothing was to be done !' " and could only be recalled to
a worthier and more helpful mood by Sterne's " pulling
off his coat and waistcoat," and "threatening to thrash
them both within an inch of their lives."

The longest journey, however, must come to an end :
and the party found much to console them at Toulouse
for the miseries of travel. They were fortunate enough
to secure one of those large old comfortable houses
which were, and, here and there, perhaps, still are
to be hired on the outskirts of provincial towns, at a
rent which would now be thought absurdly small ;
and Sterne writes in terms of high complacency of
his temporary abode. "Excellent," "well furnished,"
" elegant beyond anything I ever looked for," are some of
the expressions of praise which it draws from him : he
observes with pride that the " very great *salle à compagnie*
is as large as Baron d'Holbach's :" and he records with
great satisfaction, as well he might, that for the use of this
and of a country house two miles out of town, " besides
the enjoyment of gardens, which the landlord engaged to

keep in order," he was to pay no more than thirty pounds
a year. "All things," he adds, "are cheap in proportion :
so we shall live here for very very little."

And this, no doubt, was to Sterne a matter of some
moment at this time. The expenses of his long and
tedious journey must have been heavy : and the gold-
yielding vein of literary popularity, which he had for
three years been working, had already begun to show
signs of exhaustion. *Tristram Shandy* had lost its first
vogue ; and the fifth and sixth volumes, the copyright
of which he does not seem to have disposed of, were
"going off" but slowly.

CHAPTER VI.

LIFE IN THE SOUTH—RETURN TO ENGLAND—VOLS. VII. AND
VIII.—SECOND SET OF SERMONS.

(1762—1765.)

THE diminished appetite of the public for the humours of
Mr. Shandy and his brother is not perhaps very difficult
to understand. Time was simply doing its usual whole-
some work in sifting the false from the true—in ridding
Sterne's audience of its contingent of sham admirers. This
is not to say, of course, that there might not have been
other and better grounds for a partial withdrawal of
popular favour. A writer who systematically employs
Sterne's peculiar methods must lay his account with
undeserved loss as well as with unmerited gain. The fifth
and sixth volumes deal quite largely enough in mere
eccentricity to justify the distaste of any reader upon whom
mere eccentricity had begun to pall. But if this were
the sole explanation of the book's declining popularity, we
should have to admit that the adverse judgment of the
public had been delayed too long for justice, and had passed
over the worst to light upon the less heinous offences.
For the third volume, though its earlier pages contain some
good touches, drifts away into mere dull, uncleanly equi-
voque in its concluding chapters ; and the fifth and sixth
volumes may at any rate quite safely challenge favourable

comparison with the fourth—the poorest, I venture to think, of the whole series. There is nothing in these two later volumes to compare, for instance, with that most wearisome exercise in *double entendre*, Slawkenbergius's Tale ; nothing to match that painfully elaborated piece of low comedy, the consultation of philosophers and its episode of Phutatorius's mishap with the hot chestnut ; no such persistent resort, in short, to those mechanical methods of mirth-making upon which Sterne, throughout a great part of the fourth volume, almost exclusively relies. The humour of the fifth is, to a far larger extent, of the creative and dramatic order ; the ever-delightful collision of intellectual incongruities in the persons of the two brothers Shandy gives animation to the volume almost from beginning to end. The arrival of the news of Bobby Shandy's death, and the contrast of its reception by the philosophic father and the simple-minded uncle, form a scene of inimitable absurdity, and the "Tristrapædia," with its ingenious project for opening up innumerable "tracks of inquiry" before the mind of the pupil by sheer skill in the manipulation of the auxiliary verbs, is in the author's happiest vein. The sixth volume, again, which contains the irresistible dialogue between Mr. and Mrs. Shandy on the great question of the "Breeching of Tristram," and the much-admired, if not wholly admirable, episode of Le Fevre's death, is fully entitled to rank beside its predecessors. On the whole, therefore, it must be said that the colder reception accorded to this instalment of the novel, as compared with the previous one, can hardly he justified on sound critical grounds. But that literary shortcomings were not, in fact, the cause of *Tristram's* declining popularity may be confidently inferred from the fact that the seventh volume, with its admirably vivid and spirited scenes of Continental

travel, and the eighth and ninth, with their charming
narrative of Captain Shandy's love affair, were but slightly
more successful. The readers whom this, the third instalment
of the novel, had begun to repel, were mainly, I imagine,
those who had never felt any intelligent admiration for
the former; who had been caught by the writer's eccentricity, without appreciating his insight into character and
his graphic power, and who had seen no other aspects of
his humour than those buffooneries and puerilities which,
after first amusing, had begun in the natural course of
things, to weary them.

Meanwhile, however, and with spirits restored by the
southern warmth to that buoyancy which never long
deserted them, Sterne had begun to set to work upon a
new volume. His letters show that this was not the
seventh but the eighth; and Mr. Fitzgerald's conjecture,
that the materials ultimately given to the world in the
former volume were originally designed for another work,
appears exceedingly probable. But for some time after
his arrival at Toulouse he was unable, it would seem, to
resume his literary labours in any form. Ever liable,
through his weakly constitution, to whatever local maladies
might anywhere prevail, he had fallen ill, he writes to
Hall Stevenson, " of an epidemic vile fever which killed
hundreds about me. The physicians here," he adds, " are
the arrantest charlatans in Europe, or the most ignorant of
all pretending fools. I withdrew what was left of me out
of their hands, and recommended my affairs entirely to
Dame Nature. She (dear goddess) has saved me in
fifty different pinching bouts, and I begin to have a kind
of enthusiasm now in her favour and my own, so that one
or two more escapes will make me believe I shall leave you
all at last by translation, and not by fair death." Having

now become, "stout and foolish again as a man can wish
to be, I am," he says, "busy playing the fool with my
Uncle Toby, whom I have got soused over head and
ears in love." Now, it is not till the eighth volume that
the Widow Wadman begins to weave her spells around
Captain Shandy's ingenuous heart; while the seventh
volume is mainly composed of that series of travel-pictures
in which Sterne has manifestly recorded his own impressions
of Northern France in the person of the youthful Tristram.
It is scarcely doubtful, therefore, that it is these sketches,
and the use which he then proposed to make of them, that
he refers to, when speaking in this letter of "hints and
projects for other works." Originally intended to form a
part of the volume afterwards published as the *Sentimental
Journey*, it was found necessary, under pressure, it is to be
supposed, of insufficient matter, to work them up instead
into an interpolated seventh volume of *Tristram Shandy*.
At the moment, however, he no doubt as little foresaw this
as he did the delay which was to take place before any
continuation of the novel appeared. He clearly contem-
plated no very long absence from England. "When I
have reaped the benefit of the winter at Toulouse, I cannot
see I have anything more to do with it. Therefore, after
having gone with my wife and girl to Bagnères, I shall
return from whence I came." Already, however, one can
perceive signs of his having too presumptuously marked
out his future. "My wife wants to stay another year, to
save money; and this opposition of wishes, though it will
not be as sour as lemon, yet 'twill not be as sweet as
sugar." And, again, "if the snows will suffer me, I propose
to spend two or three months at Barége or Bagnères; but
my dear wife is against all schemes of additional expense,
which wicked propensity (though not of despotic power)

yet I cannot suffer—though, by-the-bye, laudable enough.
But she may talk; I will go my own way, and she will
acquiesce without a word of debate on the subject. Who
can say so much in praise of his wife? Few, I trow."
The tone of contemptuous amiability shows pretty clearly
that the relations between husband and wife had in nowise
improved. But wives do not always lose all their influence over husbands' wills along with the power over their
affections; and it will be seen that Sterne did *not* make
his projected winter trip to Bagnères, and that he did
remain at Toulouse for a considerable part of the second
year for which Mrs. Sterne desired to prolong their stay.
The place, however, was not to his taste; and he was not
the first traveller in France who, delighted with the gaiety
of Paris, has been disappointed at finding that French provincial towns can be as dull as dulness itself could require.
It is in the somewhat unjust mood which is commonly
begotten of disillusion that Sterne discovers the cause of his
ennui in "the eternal platitude of the French character,"
with its "little variety and no originality at all." "They are
very civil," he admits, "but civility itself so thus uniform
wearies and bodders me to death. If I do not mind I shall
grow most stupid and sententious." With such apprehensions it is not surprising that he should have eagerly welcomed any distraction that chance might offer, and in December we find him joyfully informing his chief correspondent
of the period, Mr. Foley—who to his services as Sterne's
banker seems to have added those of a most helpful and
trusted friend—that "there are a company of English
strollers arrived here who are to act comedies all the Christmas, and are now busy in making dresses and preparing some
of our best comedies." These so-called strollers were, in
fact, certain members of the English colony in Toulouse, and

their performances were among the first of those "amateur
theatrical" entertainments which now-a-days may be said
to rival the famous "morning drum-beat" of Daniel
Webster's oration, in marking the ubiquity of British
boredom, as the *reveil* does that of British power over all
the terrestrial globe. "The next week," writes Sterne,
"with a grand orchestra we play *The Busybody*, and the
Journey to London the week after; but I have some
thought of adapting it to our situation, and making it
the *Journey to Toulouse*, which, with the change of half-
a-dozen scenes, may be easily done. Thus, my dear
Foley, for want of something better we have recourse to
ourselves, and strike out the best amusements we can from
such materials." "Recourse to ourselves," however, means,
in strict accuracy, "recourse to each other;" and when the
amateur players had played themselves out, and exhausted
their powers of contributing to each others' amusement,
it is probable that "recourse to ourselves," in the exact
sense of the phrase, was found ineffective—in Sterne's
case, at any rate—to stave off *ennui*. To him, with his
copiously, if somewhat oddly furnished mind, and his
natural activity of imagination, one could hardly apply
the line of Persius,

"Tecum habita et noris quam sit tibi curta supellex;"

but it is yet evident enough that Sterne's was one of that
numerous order of intellects which are the convivial
associates, rather than the fireside companions, of their
owners, and which when deprived of the stimulus of
external excitement are apt to become very dull company
indeed. Nor does he seem to have obtained much
diversion of mind from his literary work—a form of
intellectual enjoyment which, indeed, more often pre-

supposes than begets good spirits in such temperaments
as his. He declares, it is true, that he "sports much with
my Uncle Toby" in the volume which he is now
"fabricating for the laughing part of the world ;" but if so
he must have sported only after a very desultory and
dilatory fashion. On the whole one cannot escape a
very strong impression that Sterne was heartily bored
by his sojourn in Toulouse, and that he eagerly longed for
the day of his return to "the dalliance and the wit, the
flattery and the strife," which he had left behind him in
the two great capitals in which he had shone.

His stay, however, was destined to be very prolonged.
The winter of 1762 went by, and the succeeding year had
run nearly half its course before he changed his quarters.
"The first week in June," he writes in April to
Mr. Foley, " I decamp like a patriarch with all my household, to pitch our tents for three months at the foot of the
Pyrenæan hills at Bagnères, where I expect much health
and much amusement from all corners of the earth." He
talked too at this time of spending the winter at Florence,
and, after a visit to Leghorn, returning home the following April by way of Paris ; "but this," he adds, "is a
sketch only," and it remained only a sketch. Toulouse,
however, he was in any case resolved to quit. He should
not, he said, be tempted to spend another winter there.
It did not suit his health, as he had hoped : he complained that it was too moist, and that he could not
keep clear of ague. In June, 1763, he quitted it finally
for Bagnères ; whence after a short, and, as we subsequently learn, a disappointed sojourn, he passed on to
Marseilles, and later to Aix, for both of which places he
expressed dislike ; and by October he had gone again into
winter quarters at Montpellier, where "my wife and

daughter," he writes, "purpose to stay at least a year
behind me." His own intention was to set out in
February for England, "where my heart has been fled
these six months." Here again, however, there are traces
of that periodic, or rather, perhaps, that chronic conflict
of inclination between himself and Mrs. Sterne, of which
he speaks with such a tell-tale affectation of philosophy.
" My wife," he writes in January, " returns to Toulouse,
and proposes to spend the summer at Bagnères. I, on the
contrary, go to visit my wife the church in Yorkshire.
We all live the longer, at least the happier, for having
things our own way. This is my conjugal maxim. I
own 'tis not the best of maxims, but I maintain 'tis not
the worst." It was natural enough that Sterne at any
rate should wish to turn his back on Montpellier. Again
had the unlucky invalid been attacked by a dangerous
illness ; the " sharp air " of the place disagreed with him,
and his physicians, after having him under their hands
more than a month, informed him coolly that if he stayed
any longer in Montpellier it would be fatal to him. How
soon after that somewhat late warning he took his
departure there is no record to show; but it is not
till the middle of May that we find him writing from
Paris to his daughter. And since he there announces
his intention of leaving for England in a few days, it is
a probable conjecture that he had arrived at the French
capital some fortnight or so before.

His short stay in Paris was marked by two incidents,
—trifling in themselves, but too characteristic of the
man to be omitted. Lord Hertford, the British ambas-
sador, had just taken a magnificent hotel in Paris, and
Sterne was asked to preach the first sermon in its chapel.
The message was brought him, he writes, " when I was

playing a sober game of whist with Mr. Thornhill; and
whether I was called abruptly from my afternoon amusement to prepare myself for the business on the next day,
or from what other cause, I do not pretend to determine;
but that unlucky kind of fit seized me which you know I
am never able to resist, and a very unlucky text did come
into my head." The text referred to was 2 Kings xx.
15—Hezekiah's admission of that ostentatious display of
the treasures of his palace to the ambassadors of Babylon
for which Isaiah rebuked him by prophesying the
Babylonian captivity of Judah. Nothing indeed, as
Sterne protests, could have been more innocent than the
discourse which he founded upon the *mal-à-propos* text;
but still it was unquestionably a fair subject for " chaff,"
and the preacher was rallied upon it by no less a person
than David Hume. Gossip having magnified this into
a dispute between the parson and the philosopher, Sterne
disposes of the idle story in a passage deriving an additional interest from its tribute to that sweet disposition
which had an equal charm for two men so utterly unlike
as the author of *Tristram Shandy* and the author of the
Wealth of Nations. " I should," he writes, " be exceedingly surprised to hear that David ever had an unpleasant
contention with any man; and if I should ever be made
to believe that such an event had happened, nothing
would persuade me that his opponent was not in the
wrong, for in my life did I never meet with a being of
a more placid and gentle nature; and it is this amiable
turn of his character which has given more consequence
and force to his scepticism than all the arguments
of his sophistry." The real truth of the matter was
that, meeting Sterne at Lord Hertford's table on the
day when he had preached at the Embassy Chapel,

" David was disposed to make a little merry with the parson, and in return the parson was equally disposed to make a little merry with the infidel. We laughed at one another, and the company laughed with us both." It would be absurd, of course, to identify Sterne's latitudinarian *bonhomie* with the higher order of tolerance; but many a more confirmed and notorious Gallio than the clerical humourist would have assumed prudish airs of orthodoxy in such a presence, and the incident, if it does not raise one's estimate of Sterne's dignity, displays him to us as laudably free from hypocrisy.

But the long holiday of somewhat dull travel, with its short last act of social gaiety, was drawing to a close. In the third or fourth week of May Sterne quitted Paris; and after a stay of a few weeks in London, he returned to the Yorkshire parsonage, from which he had been absent some thirty months.

Unusually long as was the interval which had elapsed since the publication of the last instalment of *Tristram Shandy*, the new one was far from ready; and even in the " sweet retirement " of Coxwold he seems to have made but slow progress with it. Indeed, the " sweet retirement " itself became soon a little tedious to him. The month of September found him already bored with work and solitude; and the fine autumn weather of 1764 set him longing for a few days' pleasure-making at what was even then the fashionable Yorkshire watering-place. " I do not think," he writes, with characteristic incoherence, to Hall Stevenson, " I do not think a week or ten days' playing the good fellow (at this very time) so abominable a thing, but if a man could get there cleverly, and every soul in his house in the mind to try what could be done in furtherance thereof I have no one to consult in these affairs. Therefore, as a man may do worse things, the plain English of all which is, that I am going to leave a few poor sheep in the wilderness for fourteen days, and from pride and naughtiness of heart to go see what is doing at Scarborough, steadfully meaning afterwards to lead a new life and strengthen my faith. Now some folks say there is much company there, and some say not ; and I believe there is neither the one nor the other, but will be both if the world will have patience for a month or so." Of his work he has not much to say : "I go on not rapidly but well enough with my Uncle Toby's amours. There is no sitting and cudgelling one's brains whilst the sun shines bright. 'Twill be all over in six or seven weeks; and there are dismal weeks enow after to endure suffocation by a brimstone fireside." He was anxious that his boon companion should join him at Scarborough ; but that additional pleasure was denied him, and he had to content himself with the usual gay society of the place. Three weeks, it seems, were passed by him in this most doubtfully judicious form of bodily and mental relaxation—weeks which he spent, he afterwards writes, in "drinking the waters, and receiving from them marvellous strength, had I not debilitated it as fast as I got it by playing the good fellow with Lord Granby and Co. too much." By the end of the month he was back again at Coxwold, "returned to my Philosophical Hut to finish *Tristram*, which I calculate will be ready for the world about Christmas, at which time I decamp from hence and fix my head-quarters at London for the winter, unless my cough pushes me forward to your metropolis" (he is writing to Foley, in Paris), "or that I can persuade some *gros milord* to make a trip to you." Again, too, in this letter we get another glimpse

at that thoroughly desentimentalized "domestic interior"
which the sentimentalist's household had long presented
to the view. Writing to request a remittance of money
to Mrs. Sterne at Montauban—a duty which, to do him
justice, he seems to have very watchfully observed—
Sterne adds his solicitation to Mr. Foley to " do some·
thing equally essential to rectify a mistake in the mind
of your correspondent there, who, it seems, gave her a
hint not long ago 'that she was separated from me for
life.' Now as this is not true in the first place, and may
fix a disadvantageous impression of her to those she
lives amongst, 'twould be unmerciful to let her or my
daughter suffer by it. So do be so good as to undeceive
him; for in a year or two she purposes (and I expect it
with impatience from her) to rejoin me."

Early in November, the two new volumes of *Shandy*
began to approach completion ; for by this time Sterne had
already made up his mind to interpolate these notes of
his French travels, which now do duty as Vol. VII. " You
will read," he tells Foley, " as odd a tour through France
as was ever projected or executed by traveller or travel-
writer since the world began. 'Tis a laughing, good-
tempered satire upon travelling—as *puppies* travel." By
the 16th of the month he had " finished my two volumes
of *Tristram*," and looked to be in London at Christmas,
" whence I have some thoughts of going to Italy this year.
At least I shall not defer it above another." On the 26th
of January, 1765 the two new volumes were given to the
world.

Shorter in length than any of the preceding instal-
ments, and filled out as it was, even so, by a process of
what would now be called " book-making," this issue will
yet bear comparison, I think, with the best of its prede-

cessors. Its sketches of travel, though destined to be
surpassed in vigour and freedom of draftsmanship, by the
Sentimental Journey, are yet excellent, and their very
obvious want of connexion with the story—if story it can
be called—is so little felt, that we almost resent the
head-and-ears introduction of Mr. Shandy and his brother,
and the corporal, in apparent concession to the popular
prejudice in favour of some sort of coherence between the
various parts of a narrative. The first seventeen chapters
are perhaps as freshly delightful reading as anything in
Sterne. They are literally filled and brimming over with
the exhilaration of travel : written, or at least prepared
for writing, we can clearly see, under the full intoxicant
effect which a bewildering succession of new sights and
sounds will produce, in a certain measure, upon the coolest
of us, and which would set a head like Sterne's in an
absolute whirl. The contagion of his high spirits is,
however, irresistible ; and putting aside all other and
more solid qualities in them, these chapters are, for mere
fun—for that kind of clever nonsense which only wins
by perfect spontaneity, and which so promptly makes
ashamed the moment spontaneity fails—unsurpassed by
anything of the same kind from the same hand. How
strange then that, with so keen an eye for the humorous, so
sound and true a judgment in the highest qualities of
humour, Sterne should think it possible for any one who
has outgrown what may be called the dirty stage of boyhood to smile at the story which begins a few chapters
afterwards—that of the Abbess and Novice of the Convent
of Andouillets. The adult male person is not so much
shocked at the coarseness of this story, as astounded at
the bathos of its introduction. It is as though some
matchless connoisseur in wine, after having a hundred

times demonstrated the unerring discrimination of his palate for the finest brands, should then produce some vile and loaded compound, and invite us to drink it with all the relish with which he seems to be swallowing it himself. This story of the Abbess and Novice almost impels us to turn back to certain earlier chapters, or former volumes, and re-examine some of the subtler passages of humour to be found there—in downright apprehension, lest we should turn out to have read these "good things," not "in," but "into" our author. The bad wine is so very bad, that we catch ourselves wondering whether the finer brands were genuine, when we see the same palate equally satisfied with both. But one should, of course, add that it is only in respect of its supposed humour that this story shakes its readers' faith in the gifts of the narrator. As a mere piece of story-telling, and even as a study in landscape and figure painting, it is quite perversely skilful. There is something almost irritating, as a waste of powers on unworthy material, in the prettiness of the picture which Sterne draws of the preparations for the departure of the two *religieuses*—the stir in the simple village, the co-operating labours of the gardener and the tailor, the carpenter and the smith, and all those other little details which bring the whole scene before the eye so vividly that Sterne may perhaps, in all seriousness, and not merely as a piece of his characteristic persiflage, have thrown in the exclamation, "I declare I am interested in this story, and wish I had been there." Nothing again could be better done than the sketch of the little good-natured "broad-set" gardener, who acted as the ladies' muleteer, and the recital of the indiscretions by which he was betrayed into temporary desertion of his duties. The whole scene is Chaucerian in its sharpness of outline and translucency of atmosphere : though there, unfortunately, the resemblance ends. Sterne's manner of saying what we now leave unsaid, is as unlike Chaucer's, and as unlike for the worse, as it can possibly be.

Still a certain amount of this element of the *non nominandum* must be compounded for, one regrets to say, in nearly every chapter that Sterne ever wrote ; and there is certainly less than the average amount of it in the seventh volume. Then again this volume contains the famous scene with the ass—the live and genuinely touching, and not the dead and fictitiously pathetic, animal ; and that perfect piece of comic dialogue—the interview between the puzzled English traveller and the French commissary of the posts. To have suggested this scene is perhaps the sole claim of the absurd fiscal system of the *Ancien régime* upon the grateful remembrance of the world. A scheme of taxation which exacted posting-charges from a traveller who proposed to continue his journey by water, possesses a natural ingredient of drollery infused into its mere vexatiousness ; but a whole volume of satire could hardly put its essential absurdity in a stronger light than is thrown upon it in the short conversation between the astonished Tristram and the officer of the fisc, who had just handed him a little bill for six livres four sous :—

"Upon what account?" said I.

"'Tis upon the part of the king," said the commissary, heaving up his shoulders.

"My good friend," quoth I, "as sure as I am I, and you are you—"

"And who are you?" he said.

"Don't puzzle me," said I. "But it is an indubitable verity," I continued, addressing myself to the commissary, changing

only the form of my asseveration, "that I owe the King of
France nothing but my good-will, for he is a very honest man,
and I wish him all the health and pastime in the world."
"Pardonnez-moi," replied the commissary. "You are indebted
to him six livres four sous for the next post from hence to St.
Fons, on your route to Avignon, which being a post royal, you
pay double for the horses and postilion, otherwise 'twould have
amounted to no more than three livres two sous."
"But I don't go by land," said I.
"You may, if you please," replied the commissary.
"Your most obedient servant," said I, making him a low
bow.
The commissary, with all the sincerity of grave good breeding,
made me one as low again. I never was more disconcerted by
a bow in my life. "The devil take the serious character of these
people," said I, aside; "they understand no more of irony
than this." The comparison was standing close by with her
panniers, but something sealed up my lips. I could not pro-
nounce the name.
"Sir," said I, collecting myself, "it is not my intention to
take post."
"But you may," said he, persisting in his first reply. "You
may if you choose."
"And I may take salt to my pickled herring if I choose.[1]
But I do not choose."
"But you must pay for it, whether you do or no."

[1] It is the penalty—I suppose the just penalty—paid by habitually extravagant humourists, that, *meaning* not being always
expected of them, it is not always sought by their readers with
sufficient care. Anyhow it may be suspected that this retort of
Tristram's is too often passed over as a mere random absurdity
designed for his interlocutor's mystification, and that its extremely
felicitous pertinence to the question in dispute is thus overlooked.
The point of it, of course, is that the business in which the commissary was then engaged was precisely analogous to that of
exacting salt dues from perverse persons who were impoverishing
the revenue by possessing herrings already pickled.

"Ay, for the salt," said I, "I know."

"And for the post, too," added he.

"Defend me!" cried I. "I travel by water. I am going down the Rhone this very afternoon; my baggage is in the boat, and I have actually paid nine livres for my passage."

"C'est tout égal—'tis all one," said he.

"Bon Dieu! What! pay for the way I go and for the way I do not go?"

"C'est tout égal," replied the commissary.

"The devil it is!" said I. "But I will go to ten thousand Bastilles first. O, England! England! thou land of liberty and climate of good-sense! thou tenderest of mothers, and gentlest of nurses!" cried I, kneeling upon one knee as I was beginning my apostrophe—when the director of Madame L. Blanc's conscience coming in at that instant, and seeing a person in black, with a face as pale as ashes, at his devotions, asked if I stood in want of the aids of the church.

"I go by water," said I, "and here's another will be for making me pay for going by oil."

The commissary of course remains obdurate, and Tristram protests that the treatment to which he is being subjected is "contrary to the law of nature, contrary to reason, contrary to the Gospel."

"But not to this," said he, putting a printed paper into my hand.

"'De par le Roi.' 'Tis a pithy prolegomenon," quoth I, and so read on. . . . . "By all which it appears," quoth I, having read it over a little too rapidly, "that if a man sets out in a post-chaise for Paris, he must go on travelling in one all the days of his life, or pay for it."

"Excuse me," said the commissary, "the spirit of the ordinance is this, that if you set out with an intention of running post from Paris to Avignon, &c., you shall not change that intention or mode of travelling without first satisfying the

fermiers for two posts further than the place you repent at; and
'tis founded," continued he, " upon this, that the revenues are
not to fall short through your fickleness."

" O, by heavens ! " cried I, " if fickleness is taxable in France,
we have nothing to do but to make the best peace we can."
And so the peace was made.

And the volume ends with the dance of villagers on " the
road between Nismes and Lunel, where is the best Muscatto
wine in all France "—that charming little idyll which won
the unwilling admiration of the least friendly of Sterne's
critics.[2]

With the close of this volume the shadowy Tristram disappears altogether from the scene ; and even the clearly-
sketched figures of Mr. and Mrs. Shandy recede somewhat
into the background. The courtship of my uncle Toby
forms the whole *motif*, and indeed almost the entire
substance of the next volume. Of this famous episode in
the novel a great deal has been said and written, and much
of the praise bestowed upon it is certainly deserved. The
artful coquetries of the fascinating widow, and the gradual
capitulation of the captain, are studied with admirable
power of humorous insight, and described with infinite grace
and skill. But there is perhaps no episode in the novel
which brings out what may be called the perversity of
Sterne's animalism in a more exasperating way. It is not so
much the amount of this element, as the time, place, and
manner in which it makes its presence felt. The senses
must of course play their part in all love affairs, except
those of the angels—or the triangles ; and such writers as
Byron, for instance, are quite free from the charge of
over-spiritualizing their description of the passion. Yet

[2] Thackeray : *English Humourists*, vol. x. p. 568, ed. 1879.

one might safely say, that there is far less to repel a
healthy mind in the poet's account of the amour of Juan
and Haidee than is to be found in many a passage in
this volume.   It is not merely that one is the poetry
and the other the prose of the sexual passion : the distinction goes deeper, and points to a fundamental difference of
attitude towards their subject in the two writers' minds.

   The success of this instalment of *Tristram Shandy*
appears to have been slightly greater than that of the
preceding one.   Writing from London, where he was
once more basking in the sunshine of social popularity,
to Garrick, then in Paris, he says (March 16, 1765),
"I have had a lucrative campaign here.   Shandy sells
well," and "I am taxing the public with two more
volumes of sermons, which will more than double the
gains of Shandy.   It goes into the world with a prancing
list *de toute la noblesse*, which will bring me in three hundred pounds, exclusive of the sale of the copy."   The
list was indeed extensive and distinguished enough to
justify the curious epithet which he applies to it ; but the
cavalcade of noble names continued to "prance" for some
considerable time without advancing.   Yet he had good
reasons, according to his own account, for wishing to
push on their publication.   His parsonage-house at Sutton
had just been burnt down through the carelessness of
one of his curate's household, with a loss to Sterne of
some 350*l.*   "As soon as I can," he says, "I must rebuild
it, but I lack the means at present."   Nevertheless, the
new sermons continued to hang fire.   Again, in April he
describes the subscription list as "the most splendid list
which ever pranced before a book since subscription
came into fashion ; " but though the volumes which it
was to usher into the world were then spoken of as about

to be printed "very soon," he has again in July to write
of them only as "forthcoming in September, though I
fear not in time to bring them with me " to Paris.   And
as a matter of fact, they do not seem to have made
their appearance until after Sterne had quitted England
on his second and last Continental journey.   The full
subscription list may have had the effect of relaxing his
energies ; but the subscribers had no reason to complain
when, in 1766, the volumes at last appeared.

The reception given to the first batch of sermons which
Sterne had published was quite favourable enough to
encourage a repetition of the experiment.   He was shrewd
enough, however, to perceive that on this second occasion
a somewhat different sort of article would be required. In
the first flush of *Tristram Shandy's* success, and in the
first piquancy of the contrast between the grave profession
of the writer and the unbounded licence of the book, he
could safely reckon on as large and curious a public for *any*
sermons whatever from the pen of Mr. Yorick.   There
was no need that the humourist in his pulpit should at all
resemble the humourist at his desk ; or, indeed, that he
should be in any way an impressive or commanding figure.
The great desire of the world was to know what he *did*
resemble in this new and incongruous position.   Men
wished to see what the queer, sly face looked like over a
velvet cushion, in the assurance that the sight would be a
strange and interesting one at any rate.   Five years afterwards, however, the case was different.   The public then
had already had one set of sermons, and had discovered
that the humorous Mr. Sterne was not a very different man
in the pulpit from the dullest and most decorous of his
brethren.   Such discoveries as these are instructive to
make, but not attractive to dwell upon ; and Sterne was

fully alive to the probability that there would be no
great demand for a volume of sermons which should only
illustrate for the second time the fact that he could be as
common-place as his neighbour.   He saw that in future
the Rev. Mr. Yorick must a little more resemble the author
of *Tristram Shandy* and it is not improbable that from
1760 onwards he composed his parochial sermons with
especial attention to this mode of qualifying them for
republication.   There is, at any rate, no slight critical
difficulty in believing that the bulk of the sermons of
1766 can be assigned to the same literary period as the
sermons of 1761.   The one set seems as manifestly to
belong to the post-Shandian as the other does to the pre-
Shandian era; and in some indeed of the apparently later
productions the daring quaintness of style and illustration
is carried so far that, except for the fact that Sterne had
no time to spare for the composition of sermons not
intended for professional use, one would have been disposed to believe that they neither were nor were meant
to be delivered from the pulpit at all.[3] Throughout all
of them, however, Sterne's new-found literary power displays itself in a vigour of expression and vivacity of illustration which at least serve to make the sermons of 1766
considerably more entertaining reading than those of 1761.
In the first of the later series, for instance—the sermon on
Shimei—a discourse in which there are no very noticeable
sallies of unclerical humour, the quality of liveliness is
very conspicuously present.   The preacher's view of the
character of Shimei, and of his behaviour to David, is
hardly that, perhaps, of a competent historical critic, and in

---

[3] Mr. Fitzgerald, indeed, asserts as a fact that some at least of
these sermons were actually composed in the capacity of *littérateur*
and not of divine,—for the press and not for the pulpit.

H

treating of the Benjamite's insults to the King of Israel he
appears to take no account of the blood-feud between the
house of David and the clan to which the railer belonged;
just as in commenting on Shimei's subsequent and most
abject submission to the victorious monarch, Sterne lays
altogether too much stress upon conduct which is indica-
tive, not so much of any exceptional meanness of disposition, as of the ordinary suppleness of the Oriental put in
fear of his life. However, it makes a more piquant and
dramatic picture to represent Shimei as a type of the
wretch of insolence and servility compact, with a tongue
ever ready to be loosed against the unfortunate, and a
knee ever ready to be bent to the strong. And thus he
moralizes on his conception:—

There is not a character in the world which has so bad an
influence upon it as this of Shimei. While power meets with
honest checks, and the evils of life with honest refuge, the world
will never be undone; but thou, Shimei, hast sapped it at both
extremes: for thou corruptest prosperity, and 'tis thou who hast
broken the heart of poverty. And so long as worthless spirits
can be ambitious ones, 'tis a character we never shall want.
Oh! it infests the court, the camp, the cabinet it infests the
church. Go where you will, in every quarter, in every profession, you see a Shimei following the wheels of the fortunate
through thick mire and clay. Haste, Shimei, haste! or thou
wilt be undone for ever. Shimei girdeth up his loins, and
speedeth after him. Behold the hand which governs everything
takes the wheel from his chariot, so that he who driveth, driveth
on heavily. Shimei doubles his speed; but 'tis the contrary
way: he flies like the wind over a sandy desert. . . . . Stay
Shimei! 'tis your patron, your friend, your benefactor, the man
who has saved you from the dunghill. 'Tis all one to Shimei.
Shimei is the barometer of every man's fortune; marks the rise
and fall of it, with all the variations from scorching hot to

freezing cold upon his countenance that the simile will admit
of.[4] Is a cloud upon thy affairs ? See, it hangs over Shimei's
brow ! Hast thou been spoken for to the king or the captain of
the host without success ? Look not into the Court Calen-
dar, the vacancy is filled in Shimei's face. Art thou in debt,
though not to Shimei ? No matter. The worst officer of the
law shall not be more insolent. What, then, Shimei, is the
fault of poverty so black ? is it of so general concern that
thou and all thy family must rise up as one man to reproach
it ? When it lost everything, did it lose the right to pity too ?
Or did he who maketh poor as well as maketh rich strip it
of its natural powers to mollify the heart and supple the
temper of your race ? Trust me you have much to answer
for. It is this treatment which it has ever met with from
spirits like yours, which has gradually taught the world to
look upon it as the greatest of evils, and shun it as the worst
disgrace. And what is it, I beseech you, what is it that
men will not do to keep clear of so sore an imputation and
punishment ? Is it not to fly from this that he rises early, late
takes rest, and eats the bread of carefulness ? that he plots,
contrives, swears, lies, shuffles, puts on all shapes, tries all gar-
ments, wears them with this or that side outward, just as it may
favour his escape ?

And though the sermon ends in orthodox fashion, with
an assurance that, in spite of the Shimeis by whom we
are surrounded, it is in our power to " lay the foundation
of our peace (where it ought to be) within our own
hearts," yet the preacher can, in the midst of his earlier
reflections, permit himself the quaintly pessimistic out-
burst : " O Shimei ! would to Heaven, when thou wast
slain, that all thy family had been slain with thee, and
not one of thy resemblance left ! But ye have multiplied

---

[4] Which are not many in the case of a *barometer.*

exceedingly, and replenished the earth ; and if I prophecy
rightly, ye will in the end subdue it.

Nowhere, however, does the man of the world reveal
himself with more strangely comical effect under the gown
of the divine, than in the sermon on " The Prodigal Son."
The repentant spendthrift has returned to his father's
house, and is about to confess his follies. But,—

Alas ! How shall he tell his story ?

Ye who have trod this round, tell me in what words he shall
give in to his father the sad items of his extravagance and
folly : the feasts and banquets which he gave to whole cities
in the east; the costs of Asiatic rarities, and of Asiatic cooks
to dress them ; the expenses of singing men and singing women ; the flute, the harp, the sackbut, and all kinds of music;
the dress of the Persian Court how magnificent ! their slaves
how numerous ! their chariots, their homes, their pictures, their
furniture, what immense sums they had devoured ! what expec-
tations from strangers of condition! what exactions! How shall
the youth make his father comprehend that he was cheated at
Damascus by one of the best men in the world ; that he had lent
a part of his substance to a friend at Nineveh, who had fled off
with it to the Ganges ; that a whore of Babylon had swallowed
his best pearl, and anointed the whole city with his balm of
Gilead ; that he had been sold by a man of honour for twenty
shekels of silver to a worker in graven images ; that the images
he had purchased produced him nothing, that they could not be
transported across the wilderness, and had been burnt with fire
at Shusan ; that the apes and peacocks which he had sent for
from Tharsis lay dead upon his hands ; that the mummies had
not been dead long enough which he had brought from Egypt ;
that all had gone wrong from the day he forsook his father's
house ?

All this, it must be admitted, is pretty lively for a
sermon. But hear the reverend gentleman once more, in

the same discourse, and observe the characteristic coolness
with which he touches, only to drop, what may be called
the "professional" moral of the parable, and glides off
into a train of interesting, but thoroughly mundane, reflections, suggested—or rather, supposed in courtesy to have
been suggested—by the text. "I know not," he says,
"whether it would be a subject of much edification to
convince you here, that our Saviour, by the Prodigal
Son, particularly pointed out those who were sinners of
the Gentiles, and were recovered by divine grace to
repentance; and that by the elder brother, he intended
manifestly the more froward of the Jews," &c. But
whether it would edify you or not, he goes on, in effect,
to say, I do not propose to provide you with edification in
that kind. "These uses have been so ably set forth in so
many good sermons upon the Prodigal Son that I shall
turn aside from them at present, and content myself with
some reflections upon that fatal passion which led him—
and so many thousands after the example—to gather all
he had together and take his journey into a far country."
In other words, "I propose to make the parable a peg
whereon to hang a few observations on (what does the
reader suppose?) the practice of sending young men
upon the Grand Tour, accompanied by a 'bear-leader,'
and herein of the various kinds of bear-leaders, and the
services which they do, and do not, render to their
charges; with a few words on society in continental cities,
and a true view of 'letters of introduction.'" That is
literally the substance of the remainder of the sermon.
And thus pleasantly does the preacher play with his
curious subject :—

But you will send an able pilot with your son—a scholar.

If wisdom can speak in no other tongue but Greek or Latin, you do well; or if mathematics will make a man a gentleman, or natural philosophy but teach him to make a bow, he may be of some service in introducing your son into good societies, and supporting him in them when he had done. But the upshot will be generally this, that on the most pressing occasions of addresses, if he is not a mere man of reading, the unhappy youth will have the tutor to carry, and not the tutor to carry him. But (let us say) you will avoid this extreme; he shall be escorted by one who knows the world, not only from books but from his own experience : a man who has been employed on such services, and thrice " made the tour of Europe with success " —that is, without breaking his own or his pupil's neck: for if he is such as my eyes have seen, some broken Swiss *valet de chambre,* some general undertaker, who will perform the journey in so many months, " if God permit," much knowledge will not accrue. Some profit, at least : he will learn the amount to a halfpenny of every stage from Calais to Rome ; he will be carried to the best inns, instructed where there is the best wine, and sup a livre cheaper than if the youth had been left to make the tour and the bargain himself. Look at our governor, I beseech you ! See he is an inch taller as he relates the advantages. And here endeth his pride, his knowledge, and his use. But when your son gets abroad, he will be taken out of his hand by his society with men of rank and letters, with whom he will pass the greatest part of his time.

So much for the bear-leader : and now a remark or two on the young man's chances of getting into good foreign society ; and then—the benediction :—

Let me observe in the first place, that company which is really good is very rare and very shy. But you have surmounted this difficulty, and procured him the best letters of recommendation to the most eminent and respectable in every capital. And I answer that he will obtain all by them which courtesy strictly stands obliged to pay on such occasions, but no more. There is nothing in which we are so much deceived as in the advantages proposed from our connexions and discourse with the literati, &c., in foreign parts, especially if the experiment is made before we are matured by years or study. Conversation is a traffic ; and if you enter it without some stock of knowledge to balance the account perpetually betwixt you, the trade drops at once; and this is the reason, however it may be boasted to the contrary, why travellers have so little (especially good) conversation with the natives, owing to their suspicion, or perhaps conviction, that there is nothing to be extracted from the conversation of young itinerants, worth the trouble of their bad language, or the interruption of their visits.

Very true, no doubt, and excellently well put ; but we seem to have got some distance, in spirit at any rate, from Luke xv. 13 : and it is with somewhat too visible effect, perhaps, that Sterne forces his way back into the orthodox routes of pulpit disquisition. The youth, disappointed with his reception by " the literati," &c., seeks " an easier society ; and as bad company is always ready, and ever lying in wait, the career is soon finished, and the poor prodigal returns—the same object of pity with the prodigal in the Gospel." Hardly a good enough " tag," perhaps, to reconcile the ear to the " And now to," &c., as a fitting close to this pointed little essay in the style of the Chesterfield Letters. There is much internal evidence to show that this so-called sermon was written either after Sterne's visit to, or during his stay in France ; and there is strong reason, I think, to suppose that it was in reality neither intended for a sermon, nor actually delivered from the pulpit.

No other of his sermons has quite so much vivacity as this. But in the famous discourse upon an unlucky text —the sermon preached at the chapel of the English

Embassy, in Paris—there are touches of unclerical raillery
not a few. Thus : " What a noise," he exclaims, " among
the simulants of the various virtues. . . Behold Humility,
become so out of mere pride ; Chastity, never once in
harm's way ; and Courage, like a Spanish soldier upon an
Italian stage—a bladder full of wind. Hush ! the sound
of that trumpet ! Let not my soldier run ! 'tis some
good Christian giving alms. O Pity, thou gentlest of
human passions ! soft and tender are thy notes, and ill
accord they with so loud an instrument."

Here again is a somewhat bold saying for a divine :—
" But, to avoid all commonplace cant as much as I can on
this head, I will forbear to say, because I do not think,
that 'tis a breach of Christian charity to think or speak
ill of our neighbour. We cannot avoid it : our opinion
must follow the evidence," &c. And a little later on,
commenting on the insinuation conveyed in Satan's question, " Does Job serve God for nought ? " he says : " It
is a bad picture, and done by a terrible master ; and yet
we are always copying it. Does a man from real conviction of heart forsake his vices ? The position is not
to be allowed. No ; his vices have forsaken him. Does
a pure virgin fear God, and say her prayers ? She is in
her climacteric ? Does humility clothe and educate the
unknown orphan ? Poverty, thou hast no genealogies.
See ! is he not the father of the child ? " In another
sermon he launches out into quaintly contemptuous criticism of a religious movement which he was certainly the
last person in the world to understand—to wit, Methodism.
He asks whether, " when a poor, disconsolated, drooping
creature is terrified from all enjoyment, prays without
ceasing till his imagination is heated, fasts and mortifies
and mopes till his body is in as bad a plight as his mind,

it is a wonder that the mechanical disturbances and con-
flicts of an empty belly, interpreted by an empty head,
should be mistook for workings of a different kind from
what they are ?" Other sermons reflect the singularly
bitter anti-Catholic feeling which was characteristic
even of indifferentism in those days—at any rate among
Whig divines. But in most of them one is liable to come
at any moment across one of those strange sallies to
which Gray alluded, when he said of the effect of Sterne's
sermons upon a reader, that " you often see him tottering
on the verge of laughter, and ready to throw his periwig
in the face of the audience."

CHAPTER VII.

FRANCE AND ITALY—MEETING WITH WIFE AND DAUGHTER—
RETURN TO ENGLAND—TRISTRAM SHANDY, VOL. IX.—
THE SENTIMENTAL JOURNEY.

(1765—1768.)

IN the first week of October, 1765, or a few days later,
Sterne set out on what was afterwards to become famous
as the "Sentimental Journey through France and Italy."
Not, of course, that all the materials for that celebrated
piece of literary travel were collected on this occasion.
From London as far as Lyons, his way lay by a route
which he had already traversed three years before, and
there is reason to believe that at least some of the scenes
in the *Sentimental Journey*, were drawn from observation
made on his former visit. His stay in Paris was shorter
this year than it had been on the previous occasion. A
month after leaving England he was at Pont Beauvoisin,
and by the middle of November he had reached Turin.
From this city he writes, with his characteristic simplicity, "I am very happy, and have found my way into
a dozen houses already. To-morrow I am to be presented
to the king, and when that ceremony is over I shall have
my hands full of engagements." From Turin he went on
by way of Milan, Parma, Piacenza, and Bologna, to Florence, where, after three days' stay, "to dine with our

Plenipo." he continued his journey to Rome. Here, and at Naples, he passed the winter of 1765—1766 :[1] and prolonged his stay in Italy until the ensuing spring was well advanced. In the month of May he was again on his way home through France, and had had a meeting after two years' separation from them, with his wife and daughter. His account of it to Hall Stevenson is curious : " Never man," he writes, " has been such a wild goose chase after his wife as I have been. After having sought her in five or six different towns, I found her at last in Franche Comté. Poor woman ! " he adds, " she was very cordial, &c." The &c. is charming. But her cordiality had evidently no tendency to deepen into any more impassioned sentiment, for she " begged to stay another year or so." As to " my Lydia," the real cause we must suspect of Sterne's having turned out of his road, she, he says, " pleases me much. I found her greatly improved in everything I wished her." As to himself : " I am most unaccountably well, and most accountably nonsensical. 'Tis at least a proof of good spirits, which is a sign and token, in these latter days, that I must take up my pen. In faith, I think I shall die with it in my hand ; but I shall live these ten years, my Antony, notwithstanding the fears of my wife, whom I left most melancholy on that account." The " fears " and the melancholy were, alas ! to be justified, rather than the " good spirits ;" and the shears of Atropos were to close, not in ten years, but in

---

[1] It was on this tour that Sterne picked up the French valet Lafleur, whom he introduced as a character into the *Sentimental Journey*, but whose subsequently published recollections of the tour (if indeed the veritable Lafleur was the author of the notes from which Scott quotes so freely) appear, as Mr. Fitzgerald has pointed out, from internal evidence to be mostly fictitious.

little more than twenty months, upon that fragile thread
of life.

By the end of June he was back again in his Yorkshire
home, and very soon after had settled down to work
upon the ninth and last volume of *Tristram Shandy.* He
was writing, however, as it should seem, under something
more than the usual distractions of a man with two
establishments. Mrs. Sterne was just then ill at Marseilles, and her husband—who, to do him justice, was
always properly solicitous for her material comfort—was
busy making provision for her to change her quarters to
Chalons. He writes to M. Panchaud, at Paris, sending
fifty pounds, and begging him to make her all further
advances that might be necessary. " I have," he says,
" such entire confidence in my wife that she spends as
little as she can, though she is confined to no particular
sum . . . . and you may rely—in case she should draw
for fifty or a hundred pounds extraordinary—that it and
every demand shall be punctually paid, and with proper
thanks ; and for this the whole Shandian family are
ready to stand security." Later on, too, he writes, that
" a young nobleman is now inaugurating a jaunt with me
for six weeks, about Christmas, to the Faubourg St.
Germain ;" and he adds—in a tone, the sincerity of which
he would himself have probably found a difficulty in
gauging—" if my wife should grow worse (having had a
very poor account of her in my daughter's last), I cannot
think of her being without me ; and, however expensive
the journey would be, I would fly to Avignon to ad-
minister consolation to her and my poor girl."[2] The

---

[2] There can be few admirers of Sterne's genius who would not
gladly incline, whenever they find it possible, to Mr. Fitzgerald's
very indulgent estimate of his disposition. But this is only one of

necessity for this flight, however, did not arise. Better accounts of Mrs. Sterne arrived a few weeks later, and the husband's consolations were not required.

Meanwhile, the idyll of Captain Shandy's love-making was gradually approaching completion : and there are signs to be met with—in the author's correspondence, that is to say, and not in the work itself—that he was somewhat impatient to be done with it, at any rate for the time. " I shall publish," he says, " late in this year ; and the next I shall begin a new work of four volumes, which when finished, I shall continue *Tristram*, with fresh spirit." The new work in four volumes (not destined to get beyond one) was of course the *Sentimental Journey.* His ninth volume of *Tristram Shandy* was finished by the end of the year, and at Christmas he came up to London, after his usual practice, to see to its publication and enjoy the honours of its reception. The book passed duly through the press, and in the last days of January was issued the announcement of its immediate appearance. Of the character of its welcome I can find no other evidence than that of Sterne himself, in a letter addressed to M. Panchaud some fortnight after the book appeared. " 'Tis liked the best of all here ;" but, with whatever accuracy this may have expressed the complimentary opinion of friends, or even the well-considered judgment of critics, one can hardly believe that it enjoyed anything like the vogue of the former volumes. Sterne, however,

many instances in which the charity of the biographer appears to me to be, if the expression may be permitted, unconscionable. I can, at any rate, find no warrant whatever in the above passage for the too kindly suggestion that " Sterne was actually negotiating a journey to Paris as ' bear-leader' to a young nobleman (an odious office to which he had special aversion), *in order* that he might with economy fly over to Avignon."

would be the less concerned for this, that his head was
at the moment full of his new venture. " I am going,"
he writes, " to publish *A Sentimental Journey through
France and Italy*. The undertaking is protected and
highly encouraged by all our noblesse. 'Tis subscribed
for at a great rate, 'twill be an original, in large quarto,
the subscription half a guinea. If you (Panchaud) can
procure me the honour of a few names of men of science,
or fashion, I shall thank you : they will appear in good
company, as all the nobility here have honoured me with
their names." As was usual with him, however, he post-
poned commencing it, until he should have returned to
Coxwold ; and, as was equally usual with him, he found
it difficult to tear himself away from the delights of
London. Moreover, there was in the present instance a
special difficulty, arising out of an affair upon which,
as it has relations with the history of Sterne's literary
work, it would be impossible, even in the most strictly
critical and least general of biographies, to observe complete silence. I refer of course to the famous and furious
flirtation with Mrs. Draper—the Eliza of the Yorick and
Eliza Letters. Of the affair itself, but little need be said.
I have already stated my own views on the general subject of Sterne's love affairs ; and I feel no inducement to
discuss the question of their innocence or otherwise in
relation to this particular amourette. I will only say that
were it technically as innocent as you please, the mean
which must be found between Thackeray's somewhat too
harsh and Mr. Fitzgerald's considerably too indulgent
judgment on it, will lie, it seems to me, decidedly nearer
to the former than to the latter's extreme. This episode
of violently sentimental philandering with an Indian
" grass widow " was, in any case, an extremely unlovely
passage in Sterne's life. On the best and most charitable

view of it, the flirtation, pursued in the way it was, and to the lengths to which it was carried, must be held to convict the elderly lover of the most deplorable levity, vanity, indiscretion, and sickly sentimentalism. It was, to say the least of it, most unbecoming in a man of Sterne's age and profession; and when it is added that Yorick's attentions to Eliza were paid in so open a fashion as to be brought by gossip to the ears of his neglected wife, then living many hundred miles away from him, its highly reprehensible character seems manifest enough in all ways.

No sooner, however, had the fascinating widow set sail, than the sentimental lover began to feel so strongly the need of a female consoler that his head seems to have softened, insensibly, even towards his wife. "I am unhappy," he writes plaintively to Lydia Sterne. "Thy mother and thyself at a distance from me—and what can compensate for such a destitution? For God's sake persuade her to come and fix in England! for life is too short to waste in separation; and while she lives in one country and I in another, many people will suppose it proceeds from choice,"—a supposition, he seems to imply, which even my scrupulously discreet conduct in her absence scarcely suffices to refute. "Besides,"—a word in which there is here almost as much virtue as in an "if,"—"I want thee near me, thou child and darling of my heart. I am in a melancholy mood, and my Lydia's eyes will smart with weeping when I tell her the cause that just now affects me." And then his sensibilities brim over, and into his daughter's ear he pours forth his lamentations over the loss of her mother's rival. "I am apprehensive the dear friend I mentioned in my last letter is going into a decline. I was with her two days ago, and I never beheld a being so altered. She has a

tender frame, and looks like a drooping lily, for the roses
are fled from her cheeks. I can never see or talk to this
incomparable woman without bursting into tears. I have
a thousand obligations to her, and I love her more than
her whole sex, if not all the world put together. She
has a delicacy," &c. &c. And after reciting a frigid
epitaph which he had written, " expressive of her modest
worth," he winds up with—" Say all that is kind of me
to thy mother; and believe me, my Lydia, that I love
thee most truly." My excuse for quoting thus fully from
this most characteristic letter, and indeed for dwelling at
all upon these closing incidents of the Yorick and Eliza
episode, is, that in their striking illustration of the soft,
weak, spiritually self-indulgent nature of the man, they
assist us far more than many pages of criticism would
do, to understand one particular aspect of his literary
idiosyncrasy. The sentimentalist of real life explains the
sentimentalist in art.

In the early days of May Sterne managed at last to tear
himself away from London and its joys, and with painful
slowness, for he was now in a wretched state of health, to
make his way back to Yorkshire. " I have got conveyed,"
he says in a distressing letter from Newark, to Hall
Stevenson, " I have got conveyed thus far like a bale of
cadaverous goods consigned to Pluto and Company, lying
in the bottom of my chaise most of the route, upon a large
pillow which I had the *prévoyance* to purchase before I
set out. I am worn out, but pass on to Barnby Moor
to-night, and if possible to York the next. I know not
what is the matter with me ; but some derangement
presses hard upon this machine. Still, I think it will not
be overset this bout "—another of those utterances of a
cheerful courage under the prostration of pain which reveal

to us the manliest side of Sterne's nature. On reaching
Coxwold his health appears to have temporarily mended,
and in June we find him giving a far better account of
himself to another of his friends. The fresh Yorkshire
air seems to have temporarily revived him, and to his
friend, Arthur Lee, a young American, he writes thus :
" I am as happy as a prince at Coxwold, and I wish you
could see in how princely a manner I live. 'Tis a land
of plenty. I sit down alone to dinner—fish and wild-
fowl, or a couple of fowls or ducks, with cream and all the
simple plenty which a rich valley under Hamilton Hills
can produce, with a clean cloth on my table, and a bottle
of wine on my right hand to drink your health. I have
a hundred hens and chickens about my yard ; and not a
parishioner catches a hare, a rabbit, or a trout, but he brings
it as an offering to me." Another of his correspondents
at this period was the Mrs. H. of his letters, whose identity
I have been unable to trace, but who is addressed in a
manner which seems to show Sterne's anxiety to expel
the old flame of Eliza's kindling by a new one. There is
little, indeed, of the sentimentalizing strain in which he
was wont to sigh at the feet of Mrs. Draper, but in its place
there is a freedom of a very prominent, and here and there
of a highly unpleasant kind. To his friends, Mr. and
Mrs. James, too, he writes frequently during this year,
chiefly to pour out his soul on the subject of Eliza ; and
Mrs. James, who is always addressed in company with her
husband, enjoys the almost unique distinction of being
the only woman outside his own family circle whom Sterne
never approaches in the language of artificial gallantry,
but always in that of simple friendship and respect.[3]

    [3] To this period of Sterne's life, it may here be remarked, is to
be assigned the dog-Latin letter ("and very sad dog-Latin too ")

I

Meanwhile, however, the *Sentimental Journey* was advancing at a reasonable rate of speed towards completion. In July he writes of himself as " now beginning to be truly busy " on it, " the pain and sorrows of this life having retarded its progress."

His wife and daughter were about to rejoin him in the autumn, and he looked forward to settling them at a hired house in York before going up to town to publish his new volumes. On the 1st of October the two ladies arrived at York, and the next day the reunited family went on to Coxwold. The meeting with the daughter gave Sterne one of the few quite innocent pleasures which he was capable of feeling ; and he writes next day to Mr. and Mrs. James in terms of high pride and satisfaction of his recovered child. " My girl has returned," he writes in the language of playful affection, " an elegant, accomplished little slut. My wife—but I hate," he adds, with remarkable presence of mind, " to praise my wife. 'Tis as much as decency will allow to praise my daughter. I suppose," he concludes, " they will return next summer to France. They leave me in a month to reside at York for the winter, and I stay at Coxwold till the 1st of January." This seems to indicate a little longer delay in the publication of

so justly animadverted upon by Thackeray, and containing a passage of which Mdme. De Medalle, it is to be charitably hoped, had no suspicion of the meaning. Mr. Fitzgerald, through an oversight in translation, and understanding Sterne to say that he himself, and not his correspondent, Hall Stevenson, was " quadraginta et plus annos natus," has referred it to an earlier date. The point, however, is of no great importance, as the untranslateable passage in the letter would be little less unseemly in 1754 or 1755 than in 1768, at the beginning of which year, since the letter is addressed from London to Hall Stevenson, then in Yorkshire, it must, in fact, have been written.

the *Sentimental Journey* than he had at first intended ; for it seems that the book was finished by the end of November. On the 28th of that month, he writes to the Earl of ——— (as his daughter's foolish mysteriousness has headed the letter), to thank him for his letter of inquiry about Yorick, and to say that Yorick "has worn out both his spirits and body with the *Sentimental Journey.* 'Tis true that an author must feel himself, or his reader will not " (how mistaken a devotion Sterne showed to this Horatian canon will be noted hereafter), "but I have torn my whole frame into pieces by my feelings. I believe the brain stands as much in need of recruiting as the body ; therefore I shall set out for town the 20th of next month, after having recruited myself at York." Then he adds the strange observation, " I might, indeed, solace myself with my wife (who is come from France), but, in fact, I have long been a sentimental being, whatever your Lordship may think to the contrary. The world has imagined because I wrote *Tristram Shandy* that I was myself more Shandian than I really ever was. 'Tis a good-natured world we live in, and we are often painted in divers colours, according to the ideas each one frames in his head." It would, perhaps, have been scarcely possible for Sterne to state his essentially unhealthy philosophy of life so concisely as in this naïve passage. The connubial affections are here, in all seriousness and good faith apparently, opposed to the sentimental emotions—as the lower to the higher. To indulge the former is to be " Shandian," that is to say, coarse and carnal ; to devote oneself to the latter, or, in other words, to spend one's days in semi-erotic languishings over the whole female sex indiscriminately, is to show spirituality and taste.

Meanwhile, however, that fragile abode of sentimentalism—that frame which had just been "torn to pieces" by the feelings, was becoming weaker than its owner supposed. Much of the exhaustion which Sterne had attributed to the violence of his literary emotions was no doubt due to the rapid decline of bodily powers which, unknown to him, were already within a few months of their final collapse. He did not set out for London on the 20th of December, as he had promised himself, for on that day he was only just recovering from "an attack of fever and bleeding at the lungs," which had confined him to his room for nearly three weeks. "I am worn down to a shadow," he writes on the 23rd, "but as my fever has left me, I set off the latter end of next week with my friend, Mr. Hall, for town." His home affairs had already been settled. Early in December it had been arranged that his wife and daughter should only remain at York during the winter, and should return to the Continent in the spring. "Mrs. Sterne's health," he writes, "is insupportable in England. She must return to France, and justice and humanity forbid me to oppose it." But separation from his wife meant separation from his daughter; it was this, of course, which was the really painful parting, and it is to the credit of Sterne's disinterestedness of affection for Lydia, that in his then state of health he brought himself to consent to her leaving him. But he recognized that it was for the advantage of her prospect of settling herself in life that she should go with her mother, who seemed "inclined to establish her in France, where she has had many advantageous offers." Nevertheless "his heart bled," as he wrote to Lee, when he thought of parting with his child. "'Twill be like the separation of soul and body, and equal to nothing but what passes at that tremendous moment; and like it in one respect, for she will be in one kingdom while I am in another." Thus was this matter settled, and by the 1st of January Sterne had arrived in London for the last time, with the first two volumes of the *Sentimental Journey.* He took up his quarters at the lodgings in Bond Street (No. 41), which he had occupied during his stay in town the previous year, and entered at once upon the arrangements for publication. These occupied two full months, and on the 27th of February the last work, as it was destined to be, of the Rev. Mr. Yorick was issued to the world.

Its success would seem to have been immediate, and was certainly great and lasting. In one sense, indeed, it was far greater than had been, or than has since been, attained by *Tristram Shandy.* The compliments which courteous Frenchmen had paid the author upon his former work, and which his simple vanity had swallowed whole and unseasoned, without the much-needed grain of salt, might, no doubt, have been repeated to him with far greater sincerity as regards the *Sentimental Journey,* had he lived to receive them. Had any Frenchman told him a year or two afterwards that the latter work was "almost as much known in Paris as in London, at least among men of condition and learning," he would very likely have been telling him no more than the truth. The *Sentimental Journey* certainly acquired what *Tristram Shandy* never did—a European reputation. It has been translated into Italian, German, Dutch, and even Polish ; and into French again and again. The French, indeed, have no doubt whatever of its being Sterne's chef-d'œuvre ; and one has only to compare a French translation of it with a rendering of *Tristram Shandy* into the same language to understand, and from our neighbours' point of view even to admit,

the justice of their preference. The charms of the
Journey, its grace, wit, and urbanity, are thoroughly congenial to that most graceful of languages, and reproduce
themselves readily enough therein; while, on the other
hand, the fantastic digressions, the elaborate mystifications,
the farcical interludes of the earlier work, appear intolerably
awkward and *bizarre* in their French dress; and what is
much more strange, even the point of the *double entendres*
is sometimes unaccountably lost. Were it not that the
genuine humour of *Tristram Shandy* in a great measure
evaporates in translation, one would be forced to admit that
the work which is the more catholic in its appeal to appreciation is the better of the two. But having regard to this
disappearance of genuine and unquestionable excellencies
in the process of translation, I see no good reason why
those Englishmen—the great majority, I imagine—who
prefer *Tristram Shandy* to the *Sentimental Journey* should
feel any misgivings as to the soundness of their taste. The
humour which goes the deepest down beneath the surface
of things is the most likely to become inextricably interwoven with those deeper fibres of associations which lie
at the roots of a language; and it may well happen, therefore, though from the cosmopolitan point of view it is a
melancholy reflection, that the merit of a book to those
who use the language in which it is written, bears a
direct ratio to the persistence of its refusal to yield up its
charm to men of another tongue.

The favour, however, with which the *Sentimental
Journey* was received abroad, and which it still enjoys
(the last French translation is very recent), is, as Mr.
Fitzgerald says, " worthily merited, if grace, nature, true
sentiment, and exquisite dramatic power be qualities that
are to find a welcome. And apart," he adds, " from these

attractions it has a unique charm of its own, a flavour, so
to speak, a fragrance that belongs to that one book alone.
Never was there such a charming series of complete little
pictures, which for delicacy seem like the series of medal-
lions done on Sèvres china which we sometimes see in old
French cabinets. . . . . The figures stand out brightly,
and in what number and variety ! Old Calais, with its
old inn ; M. Dessein, the monk, one of the most artistic
figures on literary canvas ; the charming French lady
whom M. Dessein shut into the carriage with the traveller ;
the *débonnaire* French captain, and the English travellers
returning, touched in with only a couple of strokes ; La
Fleur, the valet ; the pretty French glove-seller, whose
pulse the Sentimental one felt ; her husband, who passed
through the shop and pulled off his hat to Monsieur for the
honour he was doing him ; the little maid in the bookseller's shop, who put her little present *à part ;* the
charming Greuze 'grisset,' who sold him the ruffles ; the
reduced chevalier selling *patés ;* the groups of beggars at
Montreuil ; the *fade* Count de Bissie, who read Shakespeare ; and the crowd of minor *croquis*—postillions
landlords, notaries, soldiers, abbés, *précieuses,* maids—
merely touched, but touched with wonderful art, make
up a surprising collection of distinct and graphic
characters."

CHAPTER VIII.

(1768.)

THE end was now fast approaching. Months before, Sterne had written doubtfully of his being able to stand another winter in England, and his doubts were to be fatally justified. One can easily see, however, how the unhappy experiment came to be tried. It is possible that he might have delayed the publication of his book for a while, and taken refuge abroad from the rigours of the two remaining winter months, had it not been in the nature of his malady to conceal its deadly approaches. Consumption sported with its victim in the cruel fashion that is its wont. "I continue to mend," Sterne writes from Bond Street on the first day of the new year, "and doubt not but this with all other evils and uncertainties of life will end for the best." And for the best perhaps it did end, in the sense in which the resigned Christian uses these pious words; but this, one fears, was not the sense intended by the dying man. All through January and February he was occupied not only with business, but as it would seem with a fair amount, though less no doubt than his usual share, of pleasure also. Vastly active was he, it seems, in the great undertaking of obtaining tickets for one of Mrs. Cornely's entertainments (the "thing" to go to at that particular time) for his friends the Jameses. He writes them on Monday that he has not been a moment at rest since writing the previous day about the Soho ticket. " I have been at a Secretary of State to get one, have been upon one knee to my friend Sir George Macartney, Mr. Lascelles, and Mr. Fitzmaurice, without mentioning five more. I believe I could as soon get you a place at Court, for everybody is going ; but I will go out and try a new circle, and if you do not hear from me by a quarter to three, you may conclude I have been unfortunate in my supplications." Whether he was or was not unfortunate, history does not record. A week or two later the old round of dissipation had apparently set in. " I am now tied down neck and heels by engagements every night this week, or most joyfully would have trod the old pleasing road from Bond to Gerrard Street. . . . . I am quite well, but exhausted with a roomful of company every morning till dinner." A little later, and this momentary flash of health had died out ; and we find him writing what was his last letter to his daughter, full evidently of uneasy forebodings as to his approaching end. He speaks of "this vile influenza—be not alarmed. I think I shall get the better of it, and shall be with you both the 1st of May ;" though, he adds, " if I escape, 'twill not be for a long period, my child—unless a quiet retreat and peace of mind can restore me." But the occasion of this letter was a curious one, and a little more must be extracted from it. Lydia Sterne's letter to her father had he said, astonished him. " She (Mrs. Sterne) could know but little of my feelings to tell thee that under the supposition I should survive thy mother I should bequeath thee as a legacy to Mrs. Draper. No, my Lydia, 'tis a lady whose virtues I wish thee to imitate "—Mrs. James, in fact, whom he proceeds to praise with much and probably well-deserved warmth. "But," he adds sadly, "I think, my Lydia, thy mother will survive me ; do not deject her spirit with thy apprehensions on my account. I have sent you a necklace and buckles, and the same to your mother. My girl cannot form a wish that is in the power of her father, that he will not gratify her in ; and I cannot in justice be less kind to thy mother. I am never alone. The kindness of my friends is ever the same. I wish though I had thee to nurse me, but I am denied that. Write to me twice a week at least. God bless thee, my child, and believe me ever, ever, thy affectionate father." The despondent tone of this letter was to be only too soon justified. The "vile influenza" proved to be or became a pleurisy. On Thursday, March 10, he was bled three times, and blistered on the day after. And on the Tuesday following, in evident consciousness that his end was near, he penned that cry "for pity and pardon," as Thackeray calls it—the first as well as the last, and which sounds almost as strange as it does piteous from those mocking lips.

The physician says I am better. . . . . God knows, for I feel myself sadly wrong, and shall, if I recover, be a long while of gaining strength. Before I have gone through half the letter, I must stop to rest my weak hand a dozen times. Mr. James was so good as to call upon me yesterday. I felt emotions not to be described at the sight of him, and he overjoyed me by talking a great deal of you. Do, dear Mrs. James, entreat him to come to-morrow or next day, for perhaps I have not many days or hours to live. I want to ask a favour of him, if I find myself worse, that I shall beg of you if in this wrestling I come off conqueror. My spirits are fled. It is a bad omen ; do not weep, my dear lady. Your tears are too precious to be shed for me.

Bottle them up, and may the cork never be drawn. Dearest, kindest, gentlest, and best of women! may health, peace, and happiness prove your handmaids. If I die, cherish the remembrance of me, and forget the follies which you so often condemned, which my heart, not my head, betrayed me into. Should my child, my Lydia, want a mother, may I hope you will (if she is left parentless) take her to your bosom? You are the only woman on earth I can depend upon for such a benevolent action. I wrote to her a fortnight ago, and told her what, I trust, she will find in you. Mr. James will be a father to her. . . . . Commend me to him, as I now commend you to that Being who takes under his care the good and kind part of the world. Adieu, all grateful thanks to you and Mr. James.—From your affectionate friend,   L. STERNE.

This pathetic death-bed letter is superscribed "Tuesday." It seems to have been written on Tuesday, the 15th of March, and three days later the writer breathed his last. But two persons, strangers both, were present at his death-bed, and it is by a singularly fortunate chance therefore that one of these—and he not belonging to the class of people who usually leave behind them published records of the events of their lives—should have preserved for us an account of the closing scene. This, however, is to be found in the Memoirs of John Macdonald, "a cadet of the house of Keppoch," at that time footman to Mr. Crawford, a fashionable friend of Sterne's. His master had taken a house in Clifford Street in the spring of 1768; and "about this time," he writes, "Mr. Sterne, the celebrated author, was taken ill at the silk-bag shop in Old Bond Street. He was sometimes called Tristram Shandy and sometimes Yorick, a very great favourite of the gentlemen. One day"—namely, on the aforesaid 18th of March—"my master had company to dinner who were speaking about

him, the Duke of Roxburghe, the Earl of March, the Earl
of Ossory, the Duke of Grafton, Mr. Garrick, Mr. Hume,
and a Mr. James." Many, if not most, of the party therefore were personal friends of the man who lay dying in
the street hard by, and naturally enough the conversation
turned on his condition. " 'John,' said my master," the
narrative continues, " 'go and inquire how Mr. Sterne is to-
day.' " Macdonald did so ; and, in language which seems
to bear the stamp of truth upon it, he thus records the
grim story which he had to report to the assembled guests
on his return. "I went to Mr. Sterne's lodgings ; the
mistress opened the door. I inquired how he did ; she
told me to go up to the nurse. I went into the room, and
he was just a-dying. I waited ten minutes ; but in five
he said, ' Now it is come.' He put up his hand as if
to stop a blow, and died in a minute. The gentlemen
were all very sorry, and lamented him very much."

Thus, supported by a hired nurse, and under the curious
eyes of a stranger, Sterne breathed his last. His wife
and daughter were far away ; the convivial associates "who
were all very sorry and lamented him very much," were for
the moment represented only by "John ;" and the shock-
ing tradition goes that the alien hands by which the
"dying eyes were closed," and the "decent limbs composed, " remunerated themselves for the pious office by
abstracting the gold sleeve-links from the dead man's
wrists. One may hope indeed that this last circumstance
is to be rejected as sensational legend, but even without it
the story of Sterne's death seems sad enough, no doubt.
Yet it is, after all, only by contrast with the excited gaiety
of his daily life in London, that his end appears so forlorn.
From many a "set of residential chambers," from many
of the old and silent inns of the lawyers, departures as

lonely, or lonelier, are being made around us in London
every year : the departures of men not necessarily kinless
or friendless, but living solitary lives, and dying before
their friends or kindred can be summoned to their bed-
sides. Such deaths no doubt are often contrasted in con-
ventional pathos with that of the husband and father
surrounded by a weeping wife and children ; but the
more sensible among us construct no tragedy out of a
mode of exit which must have many times entered as at
least a possibility into the previous contemplation of the
dying man. And except, as has been said, that Sterne
associates himself in our minds with the perpetual excitements of lively companionship, there would be nothing
particularly melancholy in his end. This is subject, of
course, to the assumption that the story of his landlady
having stolen the gold sleeve-links from his dead body may
be treated as mythical ; and, rejecting this story, there
seems no good reason for making much ado about the manner of his death. Of friends, as distinguished from mere
dinner-table acquaintances, he seems to have had but few
in London : with the exception of the Jameses, one knows
not with certainty of any ; and the Jameses do not appear
to have neglected him in the illness which neither they
nor he suspected to be his last. Mr. James had paid him
a visit but a day or two before the end came : and it may
very likely have been upon his report of his friend's condition that the message of inquiry was sent from the
dinner-table at which he was a guest. No doubt Sterne's
flourish in *Tristram Shandy* about his preferring to die at
an inn, untroubled by the spectacle of " the concern of my
friends, and the last services of wiping my brows and
smoothing my pillow," was a mere piece of bravado : and
the more probably so because the reflection is appropriated

almost bodily from Bishop Burnet, who quotes it as a frequent observation of Archbishop Leighton.   But considering that Sterne was in the habit of passing nearly half of
each year alone in London lodgings, the realization of his
wish does not strike me, I confess, as so dramatically impressive a coincidence as it is sometimes represented.

According, however, to one strange story the dramatic
element gives place after Sterne's very burial to melodrama
of the darkest kind.   The funeral, which pointed after
all a far sadder moral than the death, took place on Tuesday, March 22, attended by only two mourners, one of
whom is said to have been his publisher Becket, and the
other probably Mr, James; and thus duly neglected by
the whole crowd of boon companions, the remains of
Yorick were consigned to the "new burying-ground near
Tyburn" of the parish of St. George's, Hanover Square.
In that now squalid and long-decayed grave-yard, within
sight of the Marble Arch and over against the broad ex-
panse of Hyde Park, is still to be found a tombstone in-
scribed with some inferior lines to the memory of the
departed humourist, and with a statement, inaccurate by
eight months, of the date of his death, and a year out
as to his age.   Dying, as has been seen, on the 18th of
March, 1768, at the age of fifty-four, he is declared on
this slab to have died on the 13th of November, aged fifty-
three years.   There is more excuse, however, for this want
of veracity than sepulchral inscriptions can usually plead.
The stone was erected by the pious hands of "two brother
masons," many years, it is said, after the event which it
purports to record; and from the wording of the epitaph
which commences, "Near this place lyes the body, &c.,"
it obviously does not profess to indicate—what doubtless
there was no longer any means of tracing—the exact spot

in which Sterne's remains were laid. But, wherever the
grave really was, the body interred in it, according to the
strange story to which I have referred, is no longer there.
That story goes : that two days after the burial, on the
night of the 24th of March, the corpse was stolen by
body-snatchers, and by them disposed of to M. Collignon,
Professor of Anatomy at Cambridge ; that the Professor
invited a few scientific friends to witness a demonstration,
and that among these was one who had been acquainted
with Sterne, and who fainted with horror on recognizing
in the already partially dissected "subject," the features
of his friend.   So at least this very gruesome and Poe-
like legend runs : but it must be confessed that all the
evidence which Mr. Fitzgerald has been able to collect in
its favour is of the very loosest and vaguest description.
On the other hand, it is of course only fair to recollect
that, in days when respectable surgeons and grave scientific Professors had to depend upon the assistance of
law-breakers for the prosecution of their studies and
teachings, every effort would naturally be made to hush
up any such unfortunate affair.   There is, moreover,
independent evidence to the fact that similar desecrations
of this grave-yard had of late been very common ; and
that at least one previous attempt to check the operations
of the "resurrection-men" had been attended with pecu-
liarly infelicitous results.   In the *St. James's Chronicle*
for November 26th, 1767, we find it recorded that "the
Burying Ground in Oxford Road, belonging to the Parish
of St. George's, Hanover Square, having been lately robbed
of several dead bodies, a Watcher was placed there,
attended by a large mastiff Dog ; notwithstanding which,
on Sunday night last, some Villains found means to steal
out another dead Body, and carried off the very Dog."

Body-snatchers so adroit and determined as to contrive
to make additional profit out of the actual means taken to
prevent their depredations, would certainly not have been
deterred by any considerations of prudence from attempting the theft of Sterne's corpse.   There was no such
ceremony about his funeral as would lead them to suppose
that the deceased was a person of any importance, or one
whose body could not be stolen without a risk of creating
undesirable excitement.   On the whole, therefore, it is
impossible to reject the body-snatching story as certainly
fabulous, though its truth is far from being proved : and
though I can scarcely myself subscribe to Mr. Fitzgerald's
view, that there is a " grim and lurid Shandyism " about
the scene of dissection, yet if others discover an appeal
to their sense of humour in the idea of Sterne's body
being dissected after death, I see nothing to prevent them
from holding that hypothesis as a " pious opinion."

CHAPTER IX.

STERNE AS A WRITER—THE CHARGE OF PLAGIARISM—
DR. FERRIAR'S ILLUSTRATIONS.

EVERYDAY experience suffices to show that the qualities
which win enduring fame for books and for their
authors are not always those to which they owe their
first popularity. It may with the utmost probability be
affirmed that this was the case with *Tristram Shandy*
and with Sterne. We cannot, it is true, altogether dis-
sociate the permanent attractions of the novel from those
characteristics of it which have long since ceased to
attract at all: the two are united in a greater or less
degree throughout the work; and this being so, it is of
course impossible to prove to demonstration that it was
the latter qualities, and not the former, which procured it
its immediate vogue. But, as it happens, it is possible to
show that what may be called its spurious attractions, varied
directly, and its real merits inversely, as its popularity
with the public of its day. In the higher qualities of
humour, in dramatic vigour, in skilful and subtle delinea-
tion of character, the novel showed no deterioration, but
in some instances, a marked improvement as it proceeded:
yet the second instalment was not more popular, and
most of the succeeding ones were distinctly less popular,
than the first. They had gained in many qualities,

K

while they had lost in only the single one of novelty :
and we may infer, therefore, with approximate certainty,
that what "took the town" in the first instance was,
that quality of the book which was strangest at its first
appearance. The mass of the public read, and enjoyed,
or thought they enjoyed, when they were really only
puzzled and perplexed. The wild digressions, the auda-
cious impertinences, the burlesque philosophizing, the
broad jests, the air of recondite learning, all combined to
make the book a nine-days' wonder : and a majority of
its readers would probably have been prepared to pro-
nounce *Tristram Shandy* a work as original in scheme
and conception as it was eccentric. Some there were, no
doubt, who perceived the influence of Rabelais in the
incessant digressions and the burlesque of philosophy ;
others, it may be, found a reminder of Burton in the
parade of learning : and yet a few others, the scattered
students of French facetiæ of the fourteenth and fifteenth
centuries, may have read the oroad jests with a feeling
that they had "seen something like it before." But no
single reader, no single critic of the time, appears to have
combined the knowledge necessary for tracing these three
characteristics of the novel to their respective sources :
and none certainly had any suspicion of the extent to
which the books and authors from whom they were
imitated had been laid under contribution. No one suspected that Sterne, not content with borrowing his trick
of rambling from Rabelais, and his airs of erudition from
Burton, and his fooleries from Bruscambille, had coolly
transferred whole passages from the second of these
writers, not only without acknowledgment, but with the
intention, obviously indicated by his mode of procedure,
of passing them off as his own. Nay, it was not till full

fifty years afterwards that these daring robberies were detected, or at any rate revealed to the world : and with an irony which Sterne himself would have appreciated, it was reserved for a sincere admirer of the humourist to play the part of detective. In 1812 Dr. John Ferriar published his *Illustrations of Sterne*, and the prefatory sonnet, in which he solicits pardon for his too minute investigations, is sufficient proof of the curiously reverent spirit in which he set about his damaging task.

> Sterne, for whose sake I plod through miry ways
> Of antic wit, and quibbling mazes drear,
> Let not thy shade malignant censure fear,
> If aught of inward mirth my search betrays.
> Long slept that mirth in dust of ancient days,
> Erewhile to Guise or wanton Valois dear, &c.

Thus commences Dr. Ferriar's apology, which, however, can hardly be held to cover his offence ; for, as a matter of fact, Sterne's borrowings extend to a good deal besides " mirth ;" and some of the most unscrupulous of these forced loans are raised from passages of a perfectly serious import in the originals from which they are taken.

Here, however, is the list of authors to whom Dr. Ferriar holds Sterne to have been more or less indebted : Rabelais, Beroalde de Verville, Bouchet, Bruscambille, Scarron, Swift, an author of the name or pseudonym of " Gabriel John," Burton, Bacon, Blount, Montaigne, Bishop Hall. The catalogue is a reasonably long one ; but it is not, of course, to be supposed that Sterne helped himself equally freely from every author named in it. His obligations to some of them are, as Dr. Ferriar admits, but slight. From Rabelais, besides his vagaries of narrative, Sterne took, no doubt, the idea of the *Tristra-pœdia* (by descent from the " education of Pantagruel," through

" Martinus Scriblerus ") ; but though he has appropriated
bodily the passage in which Friar John attributes the
beauty of his nose to the pectoral conformation of his
nurse, he may be said to have constructively acknowledged
the debt in a reference to one of the characters in the
Rabelaisian dialogue.[1]

Upon Beroalde, again, upon D'Aubigné, and upon
Bouchet he has made no direct and *verbatim* depredations. From Bruscambille he seems to have taken
little or nothing but the not very valuable idea of the
tedious buffoonery of Vol. iii. c. 30, et sqq. : and to
Scarron he perhaps owed the incident of the dwarf at
the theatre in the *Sentimental Journey*, an incident which,
it must be owned, he vastly improved in the taking. All
this, however, does not amount to very much, and it is
only when we come to Dr. Ferriar's collations of *Tristram
Shandy* with the *Anatomy of Melancholy*, that we begin
to understand what feats Sterne was capable of as a
plagiarist. He must, to begin with, have relied with
cynical confidence on the conviction that famous writers
are talked about and not read ; for he sets to work with
the scissors upon Burton's first page. " Man, the most
excellent and noble creature of the world, the principal

---

[1] " There is no cause but one," said my uncle Toby, " why one
man's nose is longer than another, but because that God pleases
to have it so." " That is Grangousier's solution," said my father.
" 'Tis He," continued my uncle Toby, " who makes us all, and
frames and puts us together in such forms . . . . and for such
ends as is agreeable to his infinite wisdom."—*Tristram Shandy*,
vol. iii c. 41. " Par ce, repondit Grangousier, qu'ainsi Dieu l'a
voulu, lequel nous fait en cette forme et cette fin selon divin
arbitre."—*Rabelais*, book i. c. 41. In another place, however
(vol. viii. c. 3), Sterne has borrowed a whole passage from this
French humourist without any acknowledgment at all.

and mighty work of God; wonder of nature, as Zoroaster calls him; *audacis naturæ miraculum*, the marvel of marvels, as Plato; the abridgment and epitome of the world, as Pliny," &c. Thus Burton : and, with a few additions of his own, and the substitution of Aristotle for Plato as the author of one of the descriptions, thus Sterne : " Who made MAN with powers which dart him from heaven to earth in a moment,—that great, that most excellent and noble creature of the world, the miracle of nature, as Zoroaster, in his book περὶ φύσεως, called him,—the Shekinah of the Divine Presence, as Chrysostom,—the image of God, as Moses,—the ray of Divinity, as Plato,—the marvel of marvels, as Aristotle," &c.[2]   And in the same chapter, in the " Fragment upon Whiskers," Sterne relates how a " decayed kinsman " of the Lady Baussiere " ran begging, bareheaded, on one side of her palfrey, conjuring her by the former bonds of friendship, alliance, consanguinity, &c.—cousin, aunt, sister, mother—for virtue's sake, for your own sake, for mine, for Christ's sake, remember me ! pity me !"   And again he tells how a " devout, venerable, hoary-headed man" thus beseeched her : " ' I beg for the unfortunate. Good my lady, 'tis for a prison—for an hospital; 'tis for an old man—a poor man undone by shipwreck, by suretyship, by fire. I call God and all His angels to witness, 'tis to clothe the naked, to feed the hungry,—'tis to comfort the sick and the broken-hearted.' The Lady Baussiere rode on." [3]

But now compare this passage from the *Anatomy of Melancholy* :—

A poor decayed kinsman of his sets upon him by the way,

---

[2] *Tristram Shandy*, vol. v. c. 1.   [3] *Ibid.*

in all his jollity, and runs begging, bareheaded, by him, conjuring him by those former bonds of friendship, alliance, consanguinity, &c., " Uncle, cousin, brother, father, show some pity
for Christ's sake, pity a sick man, an old man," &c. ; he cares
not—ride on : pretend sickness, inevitable loss of limbs, plead
suretyship or shipwreck, fire, common calamities, show thy
wants and imperfections, take God and all his angels to witness . . . . put up a supplication to him in the name of a thousand orphans, an hospital, a spittle, a prison, as he goes by . . . .
ride on.

Hardly a casual coincidence this. ·But it is yet more
unpleasant to find that the mock philosophic reflections
with which Mr. Shandy consoles himself on Bobby's
death, in those delightful chapters on that event, are not
taken, as they profess to be, direct from the sages of anti-
quity, but have been conveyed through, and " conveyed "
from, Burton.

" When Agrippina was told of her son's death," says
Sterne, " Tacitus informs us that, not being able to
moderate her passions, she abruptly broke off her work."
Tacitus does, it is true, inform us of this. But it was
undoubtedly Burton (*Anat. Mel.* 213) who informed Sterne
of it. So, too, when Mr. Shandy goes on to remark upon
death that " 'Tis an inevitable chance—the first statute
in Magna Charta—it is an everlasting Act of Parliament,
my dear brother—all must die," the agreement of his
views with those of Burton, who had himself said of death,
" 'Tis an inevitable chance—the first statute in Magna
Charta—an everlasting Act of Parliament—all must die," [5]
is even textually exact.

In the next passage, however, the humourist gets the
better of the plagiarist, and we are ready to forgive the
theft for the happily comic turn which he gives to it.

[4] Burton : *Anat. Mel.*, p. 269.   [5] *Ibid.*, p. 215.

Burton :—

Tully was much grieved for his daughter Tulliola's death at first, until such time that he had confirmed his mind by philosophical precepts; then he began to triumph over fortune and grief, and for her reception into heaven to be much more joyed than before he was troubled for her loss.

Sterne :—

When Tully was bereft of his daughter, at first he laid it to his heart, he listened to the voice of nature, and modulated his own unto it. O my Tullia! my daughter! my child!—Still, still, still,—'twas O my Tullia, my Tullia! Methinks I see my Tullia, I hear my Tullia, I talk with my Tullia. But as soon as he began to look into the stores of philosophy, and *consider how many excellent things might be said upon the occasion*—nobody on earth can conceive, says the great orator, how happy, how joyful it made me.

" Kingdoms and provinces, cities and towns," continues Burton, " have their periods, and are consumed." " Kingdoms and provinces, and town and cities," exclaims Mr. Shandy, throwing the sentence, like the " born orator " his son considered him, into the rhetorical interrogative, " have they not their periods ? " " Where," he proceeds, " is Troy, and Mycenæ, and Thebes, and Delos and Persepolis, and Agrigentum ? What is become, brother Toby, of Nineveh and Babylon, of Cyzicum and Mytilene ? The fairest towns that ever the sun rose upon " (and all, with the curious exception of Mytilene, enumerated by Burton) " are now no more." And then the famous consolatory letter from Servius Sulpicius to Cicero on the death of Tullia is laid under contribution—Burton's rendering of the Latin being followed almost word for word. " Returning out of Asia," declaims Mr. Shandy, " when I sailed from Ægina towards Megara " (when can this have been ?

thought my Uncle Toby), "I began to view the country round about. Ægina was behind me, Megara before," &c., and so on, down to the final reflection of the philosopher. "Remember that thou art but a man:" at which point Sterne remarks coolly, "Now, my Uncle Toby knew not that this last paragraph was an extract of Servius Sulpicius's consolatory letter to Tully "—the thing to be really known being that the paragraph was in fact Servius Sulpicius filtered through Burton. Again, and still quoting from the *Anatomy of Melancholy*, Mr. Shandy remarks how "the Thracians wept when a child was born, and feasted and made merry when a man went out of the world ; and with reason." He then goes on to lay predatory hands on that fine, sad passage in Lucian, which Burton had quoted before him : "Is it not better not to hunger at all, than to eat ? not to thirst, than to take physic to cure it ?" (why not "than to drink to satisfy thirst ?" as Lucian wrote, and Burton translated). "Is it not better to be freed from cares and agues, love and melancholy, and the other hot and cold fits of life, than, like a galled traveller who comes weary to his inn, to be bound to begin his journey afresh ?" Then, closing his Burton, and opening his Bacon at the *Essay on Death*, he adds, "There is no terror, brother Toby, in its (death's) looks, but what it borrows from groans and convulsions and " (here parody forces its way in) "the blowing of noses, and the wiping away of tears with the bottoms of curtains in a sick man's bed-room ;" and with one more theft from Burton, after Seneca : "Consider, brother Toby, when we are, death is not ; and when death is, we are not," this extraordinary cento of plagiarisms concludes.

Not that this is Sterne's only raid upon the quaint old writer of whom he has here made such free use. Several other instances of word for word appropriation might be quoted from this and the succeeding volumes of *Tristram Shandy.* The apostrophe to " blessed health " in c. xxxiii. of Vol. V. is taken direct from the *Anatomy of Melancholy;* so is the phrase, " he has a gourd for his head and a pippin for his heart," in c. ix. ; so is the jest about Franciscus Ribera's computation of the amount of cubic space required by the souls of the lost ; so is Hilarion the hermit's comparison of his body with its unruly passions to a kicking ass. And there is a passage in the *Sentimental Journey,* the " Fragment in the Abderitans," which shows, Dr. Ferriar thinks, though it does not seem to me to show conclusively, that Sterne was unaware that what he was taking from Burton had been previously taken by Burton from Lucian.

There is more excuse, in the opinion of the author of the *Illustrations* for the literary thefts of the preacher, than for those of the novelist ; since in sermons, Dr. Ferriar observes drily, " the principal matter must consist of repetitions." But it can hardly, I think, be admitted that the kind of " repetitions " to which Sterne had recourse in the pulpit—or, at any rate, in compositions ostensibly prepared for the pulpit—are quite justifiable. Professor Jebb has pointed out, in a recent volume of this series, that the description of the tortures of the Inquisition, which so deeply moved Corporal Trim in the famous Sermon on Conscience, was really the work of Bentley ; but Sterne has pilfered more freely from a divine more famous as a preacher than the great scholar whose words he appropriated on that occasion. " Then shame and grief go with her," he exclaims in his singular sermon on " The Levite and his Concubine ;" " and wherever she seeks a shelter, may the hand of justice shut the door against her !"

an exclamation which is taken, as no doubt indeed was the whole suggestion of the somewhat strange subject, from the *Contemplations* of Bishop Hall. And so, again, we find in Sterne's sermon the following :—

Mercy well becomes the heart of all Thy creatures ! but most of Thy servant, a Levite, who offers up so many daily sacrifices to Thee for the transgressions of Thy people. But to little purpose, he would add, have I served at Thy altar, where my business was to sue for mercy, had I not learned to practise it.

And in Hall's *Contemplations* the following :—

Mercy becomes well the heart of any man, but most of a Levite. He that had helped to offer so many sacrifices to God for the multitude of every Israelite's sins, saw how proportionable it was that man should not hold one sin unpardonable. He had served at the altar to no purpose, if he (whose trade was to sue for mercy) had not at all learned to practise it.

Sterne's twelfth sermon, on the Forgiveness of Injuries, is merely a diluted commentary on the conclusion of Hall's " Contemplation of Joseph." In the sixteenth sermon, the one on Shimei, we find :—

There is no small degree of malicious craft in fixing upon a season to give a mark of enmity and ill will : a word, a look, which at one time would make no impression, at another time wounds the heart, and, like a shaft flying with the wind, pierces deep, which, with its own natural force, would scarce have reached the object aimed at.

This, it is evident, is but slightly altered, and by no means for the better, from the more terse and vigorous language of the bishop :—

There is no small cruelty in the picking out of a time for mischief : that word would scarce gall at one season

which at another killeth. The same shaft flying with the wind
pierces deep, which against it can hardly find strength to stick
upright.

But enough of these *pièces de conviction.* Indict-
ments for plagiarism are often too hastily laid : but there
can be no doubt, I should imagine, in the mind of any
reasonable being upon the evidence here cited, that the
offence in this case is clearly proved. Nor, I think, can
there be much question as to its moral complexion. For
the pilferings from Bishop Hall, at any rate, no shadow
of excuse can, so far as I can see, be alleged. Sterne could
not possibly plead any better justification for borrowing
Hall's thoughts and phrases and passing them off upon
his hearers or readers as original, than he could plead for
claiming the authorship of one of the bishop's benevolent
actions and representing himself to the world as the
doer of the good deed. In the actual as in the hypo-
thetical case there is a dishonest appropriation by one
man of the credit—in the former case the intellectual, in
the latter the moral credit—belonging to another : the
offence in the actual case being aggravated by the fact
that it involves a fraud upon the purchaser of the sermon, who pays money for what he may already have in
his library. The plagiarisms from Burton stand upon a
slightly different, though not I think a much more de-
fensible footing. For in this case it has been urged, that
Sterne, being desirous of satirizing pedantry, was justified
in resorting to the actually existent writings of an antique
pedant of real life ; and that since Mr. Shandy could not
be made to talk more like himself than Burton talked
like *him,* it was artistically lawful to put Burton's exact
words into Mr. Shandy's mouth. It makes a difference,
it may be said, that Sterne is not here speaking in his

own person, as he is in his *Sermons*, but in the person of
one of his characters. This casuistry, however, does not
seem to me to be sound. Even as regards the passages
from ancient authors, which, while quoting them from
Burton, he tacitly represents to his readers as taken from
his own stores of knowledge, the excuse is hardly
sufficient; while as regards the original reflections of the
author of the *Anatomy of Melancholy* it obviously fails
to apply at all. And in any case there could be no
necessity for the omission to acknowledge the debt.
Even admitting that no more characteristic reflections
could have been composed for Mr. Shandy than were
actually to be found in Burton, art is not so exacting a
mistress as to compel the artist to plagiarize against his
will. A scrupulous writer, being also as ingenious as
Sterne, could have found some means of indicating the
source from which he was borrowing without destroying
the dramatic illusion of the scene.

But it seems clear enough that Sterne himself was
troubled by no conscientious qualms on this subject.
Perhaps the most extraordinary instance of literary
effrontery which was ever met with is the passage in
Vol. V. c. 1, which even that seasoned detective Dr.
Ferriar is startled into pronouncing "singular." Burton
had complained that writers were like apothecaries, who
" make new mixtures every day," by "pouring out of one
vessel into another." "We weave," he said, " the same
web still, twist the same rope again and again." And
Sterne *incolumi gravitate* asks : " Shall we for ever make
new books as apothecaries make new mixtures, by pouring
only out of one vessel into another ? Are we for ever
to be twisting and untwisting the same rope, for ever on
the same track, for ever at the same pace ? " And this he

writes, with the scissors actually opened in his hand for
the almost bodily abstraction of the passage beginning,
" Man, the most excellent and noble creature of the
world ! " Surely this denunciation of plagiarism by a
plagiarist on the point of setting to work could only have
been written by a man who looked upon plagiarism as a
good joke.

Apart however from the moralities of the matter, it
must in fairness be admitted that in most cases Sterne
is no servile copyist. He appropriates other men's
thoughts and phrases, and with it of course the credit
for the wit, the truth, the vigour or the learning which
characterizes them ; but he is seldom found, in *Tristram
Shandy* at any rate, to have transferred them to his own
pages out of a mere indolent inclination to save himself
the trouble of composition. He takes them less as sub-
stitutes than as groundwork for his own invention,—as
so much material for his own inventive powers to work
upon ; and those powers do generally work upon them
with conspicuous skill of elaboration. The series of
cuttings, for instance, which he makes from Burton, on
the occasion of Bobby Shandy's death, are woven into
the main tissue of the dialogue with remarkable ingenuity and naturalness ; and the bright strands of his
own unborrowed humour fly flashing across the fabric at
every transit of the shuttle. Or to change the metaphor,
we may say that in almost every instance the jewels that
so glitter in their stolen setting were cut and set by
Sterne himself. Let us allow that the most expert of
lapidaries is not justified in stealing his settings ; but let
us still not forget that the *jewels* are his, or permit our
disapproval of his laxity of principle to make us unjust
to his consummate skill.

CHAPTER X.

STYLE AND GENERAL CHARACTERISTICS — HUMOUR AND SENTIMENT.

To talk of "the style" of Sterne is almost to play one of those tricks with language of which he himself was so fond. For there is hardly any definition of the word which can make it possible to describe him as having any style at all. It is not only that he manifestly recognized no external canons whereto to conform the expression of his thoughts, but he had apparently no inclination to invent and observe, except indeed in the most negative of senses, any style of his own. The "style of Sterne," in short, is as though one should say "the form of Proteus." He was determined to be uniformly eccentric, regularly irregular, and that was all. His digressions, his asides, and his fooleries in general, would of course have in any case necessitated a certain general jerkiness of manner; but this need hardly have extended itself habitually to the structure of individual sentences, and as a matter of fact he can at times write, as he does for the most part in his *Sermons*, in a style which is not the less vigorous for being fairly correct. But as a rule his mode of expressing himself is destitute of any pretensions to precision; and in many instances it is a perfect marvel of literary slip-shod. Nor is there any ground for believing that the

slovenliness was invariably intentional. Sterne's truly
hideous French—French at which even Stratford-atte-
Bowe would have stood aghast—is in itself sufficient
evidence of a natural insensibility to grammatical accuracy. Here there can be no suspicion of designed
defiance of rules : and more than one solecism of rather a
serious kind in his use of English words and phrases
affords confirmatory testimony to the same point. His
punctuation is fearful and wonderful, even for an age in
which the *rationale* of punctuation was more imperfectly
understood than it is at present ; and this, though an
apparently slight matter, is not without value as an indi-
cation of ways of thought. But if we can hardly describe Sterne's style as being in the literary sense a style
at all, it has a very distinct *colloquial* character of its
own, and as such it is nearly as much deserving of praise
as from the literary point of view it is open to exception.
Chaotic as it is in the syntactical sense, it is a perfectly
clear vehicle for the conveyance of thought : we are as
rarely at a loss for the meaning of one of Sterne's sentences, as we are, for very different reasons, for the
meaning of one of Macaulay's. And his language is so full
of life and colour, his tone so animated and vivacious,
that we forget we are reading and not *listening*, and we
are as little disposed to be exacting in respect to form as
though we were listeners in actual fact. Sterne's manner,
in short, may be that of a bad and careless writer, but it
is the manner of a first-rate talker ; and this of course
enhances rather than detracts from the unwearying charm
of his wit and humour.

To attempt a precise and final distinction between
these two last-named qualities in Sterne or any one else
would be no very hopeful task perhaps ; but those who

have a keen perception of either find no great difficulty in discriminating, as a matter of feeling, between the two. And what is true of the qualities themselves is true, *mutatis mutandis*, of the men by whom they have been most conspicuously displayed. Some wits have been humourists also; nearly all humourists have been also wits; yet the two fall on the whole into tolerably well-marked classes, and the ordinary uncritical judgment would probably enable most men to state with sufficient certainty the class to which each famous name in the world's literature belongs. Aristophanes, Shakespeare, Cervantes, Molière, Swift, Fielding, Lamb, Richter, Carlyle : widely as these writers differ from each other in style and genius, the least skilled reader would hardly need to be told that the list which includes them all is a catalogue of humourists. And Cicero, Lucian, Pascal, Voltaire, Congreve, Pope, Sheridan, Courier, Sydney Smith—this, I suppose, would be recognized at once as an enumeration of wits. Some of these humourists, like Fielding, like Richter, like Carlyle, are always, or almost always, humourists alone. Some of these wits, like Pascal, like Pope, like Courier, are wits with no or but slight admixture of humour ; and in the classification of these there is of course no difficulty at all. But even with the wits who very often give us humour also, and with the humourists who as often delight us with their wit, we seldom find ourselves in any doubt as to the real and more essential affinities of each. It is not by the wit which he has infused into his talk, so much as by the humour with which he has delineated the character, that Shakespeare has given his Falstaff an abiding place in our memories. It is not the repartees of Benedick and Beatrice, but the immortal fatuity of Dogberry that the name of *Much*

Ado about Nothing recalls. None of the verbal quips of
Touchstone tickle us like his exquisite patronage of
William and the fascination which he exercises over the
melancholy Jacques. And it is the same throughout all
Shakespeare. It is of the humours of Bottom and Lance,
and Shallow, and Sly, and Aguecheek; it is of the
laughter that treads upon the heels of horror and pity
and awe, as we listen to the Porter in *Macbeth*, to the
Grave-digger in *Hamlet*, to the Fool in *Lear*—it is of
these that we think when we think of Shakespeare in
any other but his purely poetic mood. Whenever, that is
to say, we think of him as anything but a poet, we
think of him not as a wit, but as a humourist. So, too, it
is not the dagger-thrusts of the *Drapier's Letters*, but the
broad ridicule of the *Voyage to Laputa*, the savage irony
of the *Voyage to the Houyhnhnms*, that we associate with
the name of Swift. And conversely, it is the cold epi-
grammatic glitter of Congreve's dialogue, the fizz and
crackle of the fireworks which Sheridan serves out with
undiscriminating hand to the most insignificant of his
characters,—it is this which stamps the work of these
dramatists with characteristics far more marked than any
which belong to them in right of humorous portraiture
of human foibles or ingenious invention of comic
incident.

The place of Sterne is unmistakably among writers of
the former class. It is by his humour—his humour of
character, his dramatic as distinct from his critical de-
scriptive *personal* humour, though of course he possesses
this also as all humourists must, that he lives and will live.
In *Tristram Shandy* as in the *Sermons* there is a sufficiency of wit, and considerably more than a sufficiency of
humorous reflection, inuendo and persiflage ; but it is the

L

actors in his almost plotless drama who have established
their creator in his niche in the Temple of Fame. We
cannot indeed be sure that what has given him his hold
upon posterity is what gave him his popularity with his
contemporaries. On the contrary, it is perhaps more probable that he owed his first success with the public of his
day to those eccentricities which are for us a little too
consciously eccentric—those artifices which fail a little too
conspicuously in the *ars celandi artem*. But however
these tricks may have pleased in days when such tricks
were new, they much more often weary than divert us
now ; and I suspect that many a man whose delight in
the Corporal and his master, ih Bridget and her mistress,
is as fresh as ever, declines to accompany their creator in
those perpetual digressions into nonsense or semi-
nonsense the fashion of which Sterne borrowed from
Rabelais without Rabelais's excuse for adopting it. To
us of this day the real charm and distinction of the book
is due to the marvellous combination of vigour and
subtlety in its portrayal of character, and in the purity
and delicacy of its humour. Those last two apparently
paradoxical substantives are chosen advisedly, and employed as the most convenient way of introducing that
disagreeable question which no commentator on Sterne
can possibly shirk, but which every admirer of Sterne
must approach with reluctance. There is of course
a sense in which Sterne's humour—if indeed we may
bestow that name on the form of jocularity to which
I refer—is the very reverse of pure and delicate : a sense
in which it is impure and indelicate in the highest
degree. On this it is necessary, however briefly, to
touch ; and to the weighty and many-counted indictment
which may be framed against Sterne on this head, there

is of course but one possible plea—the plea of guilty.
Nay, the plea must go further than a mere admission of the offence ; it must include an admission of
the worst motive, the .worst spirit as animating the
offender. It is not necessary to my purpose, nor doubtless congenial to the taste of the reader, that I should
enter upon any critical analysis of this quality in the
author's work, or compare him in this respect with the
two other great humourists who have been the worst
offenders in the same way. In one of those highly interesting criticisms of English literature which, even when
they most conspicuously miss the mark, are so instructive
to Englishmen, M. Taine has instituted an elaborate comparison, very much, I need hardly say, to the advantage
of the latter, between the indecency of Swift and that of
Rabelais—that "good giant," as his countryman calls
him, "who rolls himself joyously about on his dunghill,
thinking no evil." And no doubt the world of literary
moralists will always be divided upon the question—one
mainly of national temperament—whether mere animal
spirits or serious satiric purpose is the best justification
for offences against cleanliness. It is of course only the
former theory, if either, which could possibly avail
Sterne, and it would need an unpleasantly minute
analysis of this characteristic in his writings to ascertain
how far M. Taine's eloquent defence of Rabelais could
be made applicable to his case. But the inquiry, one is
glad to think, is as unnecessary as it would be disagreeable ;
for, unfortunately for Sterne, he must be condemned on a
quantitative comparison of indecency, whatever may be
his fate when compared with these other two great writers
as regards the quality of their respective transgressions.
There can be no denying, I mean, that Sterne is of all

writers the most permeated and penetrated with impurity of thought and suggestion ; that in no other writer is its latent presence more constantly felt, even if there be any in whom it is more often openly obtruded. The unclean spirit pursues him everywhere, disfiguring his scenes of humour, demoralizing his passages of serious reflection, debasing even his sentimental interludes. His coarseness is very often as great a blot on his art as on his morality—a thing which can very rarely be said of either Swift or Rabelais ; and it is sometimes so distinctly fatal a blemish from the purely literary point of view, that one is amazed at the critical faculty which could have tolerated its presence.

But when all this has been said of Sterne's humour, it still remains true that, in another sense of the words " purity " and " delicacy " he possesses humour more pure and delicate than perhaps any other writer in the world can show. For if that humour is the purest and most delicate which is the freest from any admixture of farce, and produces its effects with the lightest touch, and the least obligations to ridiculous incident, or what may be called the " physical grotesque," in any shape—then one can point to passages from Sterne's pen which, for fulfilment of these conditions, it would be difficult to match elsewhere. Strange as it may seem, to say this of the literary Gilray who drew the portrait of Dr. Slop, and of the literary Grimaldi who tormented Phutatorius with the hot chestnut, it is nevertheless the fact, that scene after scene may be cited from *Tristram Shandy*, and those the most delightful in the book, which are not only free from even the momentary intrusion of either the clown or the caricaturist, but even from the presence of " comic properties " (as actors would call them) of any kind : scenes of which the external setting is of the simplest possible character, while the humour is of that deepest and most penetrative kind which springs from the eternal incongruities of human nature, the ever-recurring cross-purposes of human lives.

Carlyle classes Sterne with Cervantes among the great humourists of the world ; and from one, and that the most important point of view, the praise is not extravagant. By no other writer besides Sterne, perhaps, since the days of the Spanish humourist, have the vast incongruities of human character been set forth with so masterly a hand. It is in virtue of the new insight which his humour opens to us of the immensity and variety of man's life that Cervantes makes us feel that he is *great :* not delightful merely ; not even eternally delightful only, and secure of immortality through the perennial human need of joy—but *great*, but immortal in right of that which makes Shakespeare and the Greek dramatists immortal, namely, the power, not alone over the pleasure-loving part of man's nature, but over that equally universal, but more enduring element in it, his emotions of wonder and of awe. It is to this greater power—this control over a greater instinct than the human love of joy, that Cervantes owes his greatness : and it will be found, though it may seem at first a hard saying, that Sterne shares this power with Cervantes. To pass from Quixote and Sancho, to Walter and Toby Shandy involves of course a startling change of dramatic key—a notable lowering of dramatic tone. It is almost like passing from poetry to prose : it is certainly passing from the poetic in spirit and surroundings, to the profoundly prosaic in fundamental conception and in every individual detail. But those who do not allow accidental and external

dissimilarities to obscure for them the inward and essential
resemblances of things, must often, I think, have expe-
rienced from one of the Shandy dialogues the same *sort*
of impression that they derive from some of the most
nobly humorous colloquies between the knight and his
squire, and must have been conscious through all outward
differences of key and tone of a common element in each.
It is of course a resemblance of *relations*, and not of
personalities : for though there is something of the Knight
of La Mancha in Mr. Shandy, there is nothing of Sancho
about his brother. But the serio-comic game of cross-
purposes is the same between both couples ; and what
one may call the irony of human intercourse, is equally
profound, and pointed with equal subtlety, in each. In
the Spanish romance of course it is not likely to be
missed. It is enough in itself that the deranged brain
which takes windmills for giants, and carriers for knights,
and Rosinante for a Bucephalus, has fixed upon Sancho
Panza—the crowning proof of its mania—as the fitting
squire of a knight errant ! To him—to this compound of
somnolence, shrewdness, and good nature—to this creature
with no more tincture of romantic idealism than a wine-
skin, the knight addresses, without misgiving, his lofty
dissertations on the glories and the duties of chivalry—
the squire responding after his fashion. And thus these
two hold converse, contentedly incomprehensible to each
other, and with no suspicion that they are as incapable
of interchanging ideas as the inhabitants of two different
planets. With what heart-stirring mirth, and yet with
what strangely deeper feeling of the infinite variety of
human nature, do we follow their converse throughout !
Yet Quixote and Sancho are not more life-like and
human, nor nearer together at one point, and farther

apart at another, than are Walter Shandy and his brother. The squat little Spanish peasant is not more gloriously incapable of following the chivalric vagaries of his master than the simple soldier is of grasping the philosophic crotchets of his brother. Both couples are in sympathetic contact absolute and complete at one point : at another they are " poles asunder " both of them. And in both contrasts there is that sense of futility and failure, of alienation and misunderstanding—that element of under-lying pathos in short, which so strangely gives its keenest salt to humour. In both alike there is the same sugges-tion of the Infinite of disparity bounding the finite of resemblance—of the Incommensurable in man and nature beside which all minor uniformities sink into insig-nificance.

The pathetic element which underlies and deepens the humour is of course produced in the two cases in two exactly opposite ways. In both cases it is a picture of human simplicity—of a noble and artless nature out of harmony with its surroundings, which moves us ; but whereas in the Spanish romance the simplicity is that of the *incompris*, in the English novel it is that of the man with whom the *incompris* consorts. If there is pathos as well as humour, and deepening the humour, in the figure of the distraught knight-errant talking so hopelessly over the head of his attached squire's morality, so too there is pathos, giving depth to the humour of the eccentric philosopher, shooting so hopelessly wide of the intellectual appreciation of the most affectionate of brothers. One's sympathy perhaps is even more strongly appealed to in the latter than in the former case, because the effort of the good Captain to understand is far greater than that of the Don to make himself understood, and the concern of

the former at his failure is proportionately more marked
than that of the latter at *his*. And the general *rapport*
between one of the two ill-assorted pairs is much closer
than that of the other. It is, indeed, the tantalizing
approach to a mutual understanding, which gives so much
more subtle a zest to the humour of the relations between
the two brothers Shandy than to that which arises out of
the relations between the philosopher and his wife. The
broad comedy of the dialogues between Mr. and Mrs.
Shandy is irresistible in its way : but it *is* broad comedy.
The philosopher knows that his wife does not comprehend
him : she knows that she never will ; and neither of
them much cares. The husband snubs her openly for
her mental defects ; and she with perfect placidity accepts
his rebukes. " Master," as he once complains, " of one
of the finest chains of reasoning in the world, he is unable
for the soul of him to get a single link of it into the head
of his wife ;" but we never hear him lamenting in this
serio-comic fashion over his brother's inability to follow
his processes of reasoning. That is too serious a matter
with both of them ; their mutual desire to share each
other's ideas and tastes, is too strong : and each time that
the philosopher shows his impatience with the soldier's
fortification-hobby, or the soldier breaks his honest shins
over one of the philosopher's crotchets, the regret and
remorse on either side is equally acute and sincere. It
must be admitted, however, that Captain Shandy is the
one who the more frequently subjects himself to pangs of
this sort, and who is the more innocent sufferer of the
two.

From the broad and deep humour of this central
conception of contrast, flow as from a head-water innumerable rills of comedy, through many and many a

page of dialogue; but not, of course, from this source
alone. Uncle Toby is ever delightful, even when his
brother is not near him as his foil: the faithful corporal
brings out another side of his character, upon which we
linger with equal pleasure of contemplation : the allure-
ments of the Widow Wadman reveal him to us in yet
another—but always in a captivating aspect. There is
too, one need hardly say, an abundance of humour, of a
high, though not the highest order, in the minor characters of the story—in Mrs. Shandy, in the fascinating
widow, and even, under the coarse lines of the physical
caricature, in the keen little Catholic, Slop himself. But
it is in Toby Shandy alone that humour reaches that
supreme level which it is only capable of attaining when
the collision of contrasted qualities in a human character
produce a corresponding conflict of the emotions of mirth
and tenderness in the minds of those who contemplate it.

This, however, belongs more rightfully to the consideration of the creative and dramatic element in Sterne's
genius ; and an earlier place in the analysis is claimed by
that power over the emotion of pity upon which Sterne,
beyond question, prided himself more highly than upon
any other of his gifts. He preferred, we can plainly see,
to think of himself, not as the great humourist, but as the
great sentimentalist : and though the word "sentiment"
had something even in *his* day of the depreciatory meaning which distinguishes it nowadays from "pathos," there
can be little doubt that the thing appeared to Sterne to
be on the whole, and both in life and literature, rather
admirable than the reverse.

What then were his notions of true "sentiment" in
literature ? We have seen elsewhere that he repeats,
it would appear unconsciously, and commends the canon

which Horace propounds to the tragic poet, in the
words,—

Si vis me flere, dolendum
Primum ipsi tibi : tunc tua me infortunia lædent.

And that canon is sound enough, no doubt, in the sense
in which it was meant, and in its relation to the person to
whom it was addressed. A tragic drama, peopled with
heroes who set forth their woes in frigid and unim-
passioned verse, will unquestionably leave its audience as
cold as itself. Nor is this true of drama alone. All *poetry*
indeed, whether dramatic or other, presupposes a sympathetic unity of emotion between the poet and those whom
he addresses ; and to this extent it is obviously true that
he must feel before they can. Horace, who was (what
every literary critic is not) a man of the world and an
observer of human nature, did not of course mean that
this capacity for feeling was all, or even the chief part of
the poetic faculty. He must have seen many an "intense"
young Roman make that pathetic error of the young in
all countries and of all periods—the error of mistaking the
capacity of emotion for the gift of expression. He did, however, undoubtedly mean that a poet's power of affecting
others presupposes passion in himself ; and as regards the
poet he was right. But his criticism takes no account
whatever of one form of appeal to the emotions which has
been brought by later art to a high pitch of perfection,
but with which the personal feeling of the artist has not
much more to do than the " passions " of an auctioneer's
clerk have to do with the compilation of his inventory. A
poet himself, Horace wrote for poets : to him the pathetic
implied the ideal, the imaginative, the rhetorical ; he lived
before the age of Realism and the Realists, and would
scarcely have comprehended either the men or the method

if he could have come across them. Had he done so, however, he would have been astonished to find his canon
reversed, and to have perceived that the primary condition
of the Realist's success, and the distinctive note of those
writers who have pressed genius into the service of Realism,
is that they do *not* share—that they are unalterably and
ostentatiously free from—the emotions to which they
appeal in their readers. A fortunate accident has enabled
us to compare the treatment which the world's greatest
tragic poet and its greatest master of realistic tragedy have
respectively applied to virtually the same subject ; and
the two methods are never likely to be again so impres-
sively contrasted as in *King Lear* and *Le Père Goriot.*
But, in truth, it must be impossible for any one who feels
Balzac's power not to feel also how it is heightened by
Balzac's absolute calm—a calm entirely different from that
stern composure which was merely a point of style and
not an attitude of the heart with the old Greek tragedians—a calm which, unlike theirs, insulates, so to speak,
and is intended to insulate the writer, to the end that his
individuality, of which only the electric current of sympathy ever makes a reader conscious, may disappear, and
the characters of the drama stand forth the more life-like
from the complete concealment of the hand that moves
them.

Of this kind of art Horace, as has been said, knew
nothing, and his canon only applies to it by the rule
of contraries. Undoubtedly, and in spite of the marvels
which one great genius has wrought with it, it is a form
lower than the poetic—essentially a prosaic, and in many
or most hands an unimaginative form of art; but for this
very reason, that it demands nothing of its average practitioner but a keen eye for facts great and small, and

a knack of graphically recording them, it has become a
far more commonly and successfully cultivated form of
art than any other. As to the question who *are* its
practitioners, it would, of course, be the merest dog-
matism to commit oneself to any attempt at rigid classification in such a matter. There are few if any writers
who can be described without qualification either as
Realists or as Idealists. Nearly all of them, probably, are
Realists at one moment and in one mood, and Idealists
at other moments and in other moods. All that need be
insisted on is that the methods of the two forms of art
are essentially distinct, and that artistic failure must result
from any attempt to combine them ; for, whereas the
primary condition of success in the one case is that the
reader should feel the sympathetic presence of the writer,
the primary condition of success in the other is that the
writer should efface himself from the reader's consciousness
altogether. And it is, I think, the defiance of these conditions which explains why so much of Sterne's deliberately pathetic writing is, from the artistic point of view,
a failure. It is this which makes one feel so much of it
to be strained and unnatural, and which brings it to pass
that some of his most ambitious efforts leave the reader
indifferent, or even now and then contemptuous. In
those passages of pathos in which the effect is distinctly
sought by realistic means, Sterne is perpetually ignoring
the " self-denying ordinance " of his adopted method—
perpetually obtruding his own individuality, and begging
us, as it were, to turn from the picture to the artist, to
cease gazing for a moment at his touching creation, and
to admire the fine feeling, the exquisitely sympathetic
nature of the man who created it. No doubt, as we must
in fairness remember, it was part of his " humour "—in

Ancient Pistol's sense of the word—to do this ; it is true, no doubt (and a truth which Sterne's most famous critic was too prone to ignore) that his sentiment is not always *meant* for serious ;[1] nay, the very word "sentimental" itself, though in Sterne's day, of course, it had acquired but a part of its present disparaging significance, is a sufficient proof of that. But there are, nevertheless, plenty of passages, both in *Tristram Shandy* and the *Sentimental Journey*, where the intention is wholly and unmixedly pathetic—where the smile is not for a moment meant to compete with the tear, which are nevertheless, it must be owned, complete failures, and failures traceable with much certainty, or so it seems to me, to the artistic error above-mentioned.

In one famous case, indeed, the failure can hardly be described as other than ludicrous, The figure of the distraught Maria of Moulines is tenderly drawn ; the accessories of the picture—her goat, her dog, her pipe, her song to the Virgin—though a little theatrical perhaps, are skilfully touched in ; and so long as the Sentimental Traveller keeps our attention fixed upon her and them the scene prospers well enough. But after having bidden us duly note how "the tears trickled down her

---

[1] Surely it was not so meant, for instance, in the passage about the *désobligeante*, which had been "standing so many months unpitied in the corner of Monsieur Dessein's coach-yard. Much, indeed, was not to be said for it, but something might ; and when a few words will rescue Misery out of her distress, I hate the man who can be a churl of them." "Does anybody," asks Thackeray in strangely matter-of-fact fashion, "believe that this is a real sentiment ? that this luxury of generosity, this gallant rescue of Misery—out of an old cab—is genuine feeling ?" Nobody, we should say. But, on the other hand, does anybody—or did anybody before Thackeray—suggest that it was meant to pass for genuine feeling ? Is it not an obvious piece of mock pathetic ?

cheeks," the Traveller continues : " I sat down close
by her, and Maria let me wipe them away as they
fell, with my handkerchief. I then steeped it in my
own—and then in hers—and then in mine—and then
I wiped hers again ; and as I did it, I felt such un-
describable emotions within me as I am sure could not
be accounted for from any combinations of matter and
motion." The reader of this may well ask himself in
wonderment whether he is really expected to make a
third in the lachrymose group. We look at the passage
again, and more carefully, to see if after all we may not
be intended to laugh, and not to cry at it ; but on finding,
as clearly appears, that we actually *are* intended to cry at
it, the temptation to laugh becomes **almost** irresistible.
We proceed, however, to the account of Maria's wanderings
to Rome and back, and we come to the pretty passage
which follows :—

How she had borne it, and how she had got supported, she
could not tell; but God tempers the winds, said Maria, to the
shorn lamb. Shorn indeed ! and to the quick, said I ; and
wast thou in my own land, where I have a cottage, I would take
thee to it, and shelter thee; thou shouldst eat of my own bread
and drink of my own cup ; I would be kind to thy Sylvio ; in
all thy weaknesses and wanderings I would seek after thee, and
bring thee back. When the sun went down I would say my
prayers; and when I had done thou shouldst play thy evening-
song upon thy pipe : nor would the incense of my sacrifice be
worse accepted for entering heaven along with that of a broken
heart."

But then follows more whimpering :—

Nature melted within me [continues Sterne] as I said this ;
and Maria observing, as I took out my handkerchief, that it
was steeped too much already to be of use, would needs go wash

it in the stream. And where will you dry it, Maria? said I.
I'll dry it in my bosom, said she; 'twill do me good. And is
your heart still so warm, Maria? said I. I touched upon the
string on which hung all her sorrows. She looked with wistful
disorder for some time in my face; and then, without saying
anything, took her pipe and played her service to the Virgin.

Which are we meant to look at—the sorrows of Maria?
or the sensibilities of the Sentimental Traveller? or the condition of the pocket-handkerchief? I think it doubtful
whether any writer of the first rank has ever perpetrated
so disastrous a literary failure as this scene; but the main
cause of that failure appears to me not doubtful at all.
The artist has no business within the frame of the picture,
and his intrusion into it has spoilt it. The method adopted
from the commencement is ostentatiously objective: we
are taken straight into Maria's presence, and bidden to
look at and to pity the unhappy maiden as *described* by
the Traveller who met her. No attempt is made to place
us at the outset in sympathy with *him;* he, until he thrusts
himself before us with his streaming eyes, and his drenched
pocket-handkerchief, is a mere reporter of the scene before
him, and he and his tears are as much out of place as if he
were the compositor who set up the type. It is not merely
that we don't want to know how the scene affected him,
and that we resent as an impertinence the elaborate
account of his tender emotions; we don't wish to be
reminded of his presence at all. For as we can know
nothing (effectively) of Maria's sorrows except as given
in her appearance, the historical recital of them and their
cause being too curt and bald to be able to move us—the
best chance of moving our compassion for her is to make
the illusion of her presence as dramatically real as possible;
a chance which is therefore completely destroyed when

the author of the illusion insists on thrusting himself
between ourselves and the scene.

But in truth this whole episode of Maria of Moulines
was, like more than one of Sterne's efforts after the
pathetic, condemned to failure from the very conditions
of its birth. These abortive efforts are no natural growth
of his artistic genius ; they proceed rather from certain
morbidly stimulated impulses of his moral nature which
he forced his artistic genius to subserve. He had true
pathetic power, simple yet subtle, at his command ; but
it visited him unsought, and by inspiration from without.
It came when he was in the dramatic and not in the
introspective mood ; when he was thinking honestly of
his characters and not of himself. But he was unfortunately too prone—and a long course of moral self-
indulgence had confirmed him in it—to the habit of
caressing his own sensibilities ; and the result of this
was always to set him upon one of those attempts to be
pathetic of malice prepense of which Maria of Moulines
is one example, and the too celebrated dead donkey of
Nampont another. "It is agreeably and skilfully done,
that dead jackass," writes Thackeray ; "like M. de
Soubise's cook on the campaign, Sterne dresses it, and
serves it up quite tender, and with a very piquante sauce.
But tears, and fine feelings, and a white pocket-handkerchief, and a funeral sermon, and horses and feathers,
and a procession of mutes, and a hearse with a dead
donkey inside. Psha ! Mountebank ! I'll not give thee
one penny-piece for that trick, donkey and all." That
is vigorous ridicule, and not wholly undeserved ; but
on the other hand, not entirely deserved. There is less
of artistic trick, it seems to me, and more of natural foible,
about Sterne's literary sentiment than Thackeray was

ever willing to believe ; and I can find nothing worse,
though nothing better, in the dead ass of Nampont than in
Maria of Moulines. I do not think there is any conscious simulation of feeling in this Nampont scene : it
is that the feeling itself is overstrained—that Sterne,
hugging as usual his own sensibilities, mistook their
value in expression for the purposes of art. The Sentimental Traveller does not obtrude himself to the same
extent as in the scene at Moulines : but a little consideration of the scene will show how much Sterne relied
on the mere presentment of the fact that here was an
unfortunate peasant who had lost his dumb companion,
and here a tender-hearted gentleman looking on and
pitying him. As for any attempts to bring out by
objective dramatic touches, either the grievousness of the
bereavement or the grief of the mourner, such attempts
as are made to do this are either commonplace, or " one
step in advance " of the sublime. Take this for instance :
" The mourner was sitting upon a stone bench at the
door, with his ass's pannel and its bridle on one side,
which he took up from time to time, then laid them
down, looked at them, and shook his head. He then
took the crust of bread out of his wallet again, as if
to eat it : held it some time in his hand, then laid it
upon the bit of his ass's bridle—looked wistfully at the
little arrangement he had made—and then gave a sigh.
The simplicity of his grief drew numbers about him,"
&c. Simplicity indeed of a marvellous sort which could
show itself by so extraordinary a piece of acting as this !
Is there any critic who candidly thinks it natural—I do
not mean in the sense of mere everyday probability, but
of conformity to the laws of human character ? Is it true
that in any country, among any people however emotional,

M

grief—real, unaffected, un-selfconscious grief—ever did or
ever could display itself by such a trick as that of laying
a piece of bread on the bit of a dead ass's bridle ? Do
we not feel that if we had been on the point of offering
comfort or alms to the mourner, and saw him go through
this extraordinary piece of pantomime, we should have
buttoned up our hearts and our pockets forthwith ?
Sentiment again sails very near the wind of the ludicrous
in the reply to the traveller's remark that the mourner
had been a merciful master to the dead ass. "Alas!" the
latter says, "I thought so when he was alive, but now that
he is dead I think otherwise. I fear the weight of *myself
and my afflictions* have been too much for him." And
the scene ends flatly enough with the scrap of morality.
"Shame on the world! said I to myself. Did we love
each other as this poor soul loved his ass, 'twould be
something."

The whole incident, in short, is one of those examples of the deliberate-pathetic with which Sterne's
highly natural art had least, and his highly artificial
nature most, to do. He is never so unsuccessful as when,
after formally announcing as it were that he means to be
touching, he proceeds to select his subject, to marshal
his characters, to group his accessories, and with painful
and painfully apparent elaboration to work up his scene
to the weeping point. There is no obviousness of
suggestion, no spontaneity of treatment about this "Dead
Ass" episode : indeed, there is some reason to believe
that it was one of those most hopeless of efforts—the
attempt at the mechanical repetition of a former triumph.
It is by no means improbable at any rate that the dead
ass of Nampont owes its presence in the *Sentimental
Journey* to the reception met with by the live ass of

Lyons in the seventh volume of *Tristram Shandy*. And
yet what an astonishing difference between the two
sketches !

'Twas a poor ass, who had just turned in with a couple of
large panniers upon his back, to collect eleemosynary turnip-tops
and cabbage-leaves, and stood dubious with his two fore-feet on
the inside of the threshold, and with his two hinder feet towards
the street, as not knowing very well whether he would go in or
no. Now, 'tis an animal (be in what hurry I may) I cannot
bear to strike. There is a patient endurance of sufferings
wrote so unaffectedly in his looks and carriage, which pleads so
mightily for him that it always disarms me, and to that degree
that I do not like to speak unkindly to him ; on the contrary,
meet him where I will, in town or country, in cart or under
panniers, whether in liberty or bondage, I have ever something
civil to say to him on my part ; and as one word begets another
(if he has as little to do as I) I generally fall into conversation
with him ; and surely never is my imagination so busy as in
framing his responses from the etchings of his countenance—and
where those carry me not deep enough, in flying from my own
heart into his, and feeling what is natural for an ass to think,
as well as a man, upon the occasion. . . . . Come, Honesty !
said I, seeing it was impracticable to pass betwixt him and the
gate, art thou for coming in or going out ? The ass twisted his
head round, to look up the street. Well, replied I, we'll wait a
minute for thy driver. He turned his head thoughtfully about,
and looked wistfully the opposite way. I understand thee perfectly, answered I ; if thou takest a wrong step in this affair he
will cudgel thee to death. Well, a minute is but a minute, and
if it saves a fellow-creature a drubbing, it shall not be set down
as ill spent. He was eating the stem of an artichoke as this
discourse went on, and in the little peevish contentions of
nature betwixt hunger and unsavouriness, had dropped it out of
his mouth half a dozen times, and picked it up again. God help
thee, Jack ! said I, thou hast a bitter breakfast on't, and many
a bitter day's labour, and many a bitter blow, I fear, for its

wages—'tis all, all bitterness to thee, whatever life is to others.
And now thy mouth, if one knew the truth of it, is as bitter, I
dare say, as soot (for he had cast aside the stem), and thou hast
not a friend perhaps in all this world that will give thee a
macaroon.   In saying this, I pulled out a paper of 'em, which I
had just purchased, and gave him one ; and, at this moment that
I am telling it, my heart smites me that there was more of
pleasantry in the conceit of seeing how an ass would eat a
macaroon, than of benevolence in giving him one, which presided
in the act.   When the ass had eaten his macaroon, I pressed
him to come in.   The poor beast was heavy loaded, his legs
seemed to tremble under him, he hung rather backwards, and
as I pulled at his halter it broke short in my hand.   He looked
up pensive in my face.   " Don't thrash me with it ; but, if you
will, you may."   " If I do," said I, " I'll be d——d."

Well might Thackeray say of this passage that, " the
critic who refuses to see in it wit, humour, pathos, a
kind nature speaking, and a real sentiment, must be hard
indeed to move and to please."   It is, in truth, excellent ;
and its excellence is due to its possessing nearly every
one of those qualities, positive and negative, which the
two other scenes above quoted are without.   The author
does not here obtrude himself, does not importune us to
admire his exquisitely compassionate nature : on the
contrary, he at once amuses us and enlists our sympathies
by that subtly humorous piece of self-analysis, in which
he shows how large an admixture of curiosity was contained in his benevolence.   The incident, too, is well
chosen.   No forced concurrence of circumstances brings it
about : it is such as any man might have met with
anywhere in his travels, and it is handled in a simple
and manly fashion.   The reader is *with* the writer
throughout : and their common mood of half-humorous
pity is sustained, unforced, but unbroken from first to last.

One can hardly say as much for another of the much

quoted pieces from the *Sentimental Journey*—the description of the caged starling. The passage is in-
geniously worked into its context; and if we were to
consider it as only intended to serve the purpose of a
sudden and dramatic discomfiture of the traveller's somewhat inconsiderate moralizings on captivity, it would be
well enough. But regarded as a substantive appeal to
one's emotions, it is open to the criticisms which apply to
most other of Sterne's too deliberate attempts at the
pathetic. The details of the picture are too much insisted on, and there is too much of self-consciousness in
the artist. Even at the very close of the story of
Lefevre's death, finely told though, as a whole, it is, there
is a jarring note. Even while the dying man is breathing
his last, our sleeve is twitched as we stand at his bedside,
and our attention forcibly diverted from the departing
soldier to the literary ingenuities of the man who is
describing his end.

> There was a frankness in my uncle Toby, not the effect of
> familiarity, but the cause of it, which let you at once into his
> soul, and showed you the goodness of his nature. To this there
> was something in his looks, and voice, and manner, superadded,
> which eternally beckoned to the unfortunate to come and take
> shelter under him; so that, before my uncle Toby had half
> finished the kind offers he was making to the father, had the
> son insensibly pressed up close to his knees, and had taken hold
> of the breast of his coat, and was pulling it towards him. The
> blood and spirits of Le Fevre, which were waxing cold and slow
> within him, and were retreating to their last citadel, the heart,
> rallied back : the film forsook his eyes far a moment ; he looked
> up wishfully in my uncle Toby's face, then cast a look upon his
> boy ;—and that ligament, fine as it was, was never broken.

How excellent all that is ! and how perfectly would
the scene have ended had it closed with the tender and

poetic image which thus describes the dying soldier's commendation of his orphan boy to the care of his brother-in-arms ! But what of this, which closes the scene in fact ?

Nature instantly ebbed again ; the film returned to its place ; the pulse fluttered—stopped—went on—throbbed—stopped again—moved, stopped. Shall I go on ? No.

Let those admire this who can. To me I confess it seems to spoil a touching and simple death-bed scene by a piece of theatrical trickery.

The sum in fact of the whole matter appears to be, that the sentiment on which Sterne so prided himself—the acute sensibilities which he regarded with such extraordinary complacency, were, as has been before observed, the weakness and not the strength of his pathetic style. When Sterne the artist is uppermost, when he is surveying his characters with that penetrating eye of his, and above all when he is allowing his subtle and tender humour to play upon them unrestrained, he can touch the springs of compassionate emotion in us with a potent and unerring hand. But when Sterne the man is uppermost —when he is looking inward and not outward, contemplating his own feelings instead of those of his personages, his cunning fails him altogether. He is at his best in pathos, when he is most the humourist : or rather, we may almost say his pathos is never good unless when it is closely interwoven with his humour. In this of course there is nothing at all surprising. The only marvel is, that a man who was such a master of the humorous in its highest and deepest sense, should seem to have so little understood how near together lie the sources of tears and laughter on the very way-side of man's mysterious life.

CHAPTER XI.

CREATIVE AND DRAMATIC POWER—PLACE IN ENGLISH
LITERATURE.

SUBTLE as is Sterne's humour, and true as, in its proper
moods, is his pathos, it is not to these but to the parent
gift from which they sprang, and perhaps to only one
special display of that gift, that he owes his immortality.
We are accustomed to bestow so lightly this last hyperbolic honour—hyperbolic always, even when we are
speaking of a Homer or a Shakespeare, if only we project
the vision far enough forward through time—that the
comparative ease with which it is to be earned has itself
come to be exaggerated. There are so many "deathless
ones" about—if I may put the matter familiarly—in
conversation and in literature, that we get into the
way of thinking that they are really a considerable
body in actual fact, and that the works which have
triumphed over death are far more numerous still. The
real truth, however, is, that not only are "those who
reach posterity a very select company indeed;" but most
of them have come much nearer missing their destiny
than is popularly supposed. Of the dozen or score of
writers in one century whom their own contemporaries
fondly decree immortal, one-half perhaps may be remembered in the next; while of the creations which were
honoured with the diploma of immortality a very much

smaller proportion as a rule survive. Only some fifty
per cent. of the prematurely laurel-crowned reach the
goal; and often, even upon *their* brows there flutter but
a few stray leaves of the bay. A single poem, a solitary
drama—nay, perhaps one isolated figure, poetic or dramatic—avails, and but barely avails, to keep the immortal
from putting on mortality. Hence we need think it no
disparagement to Sterne to say that he lives not so much
in virtue of his creative power as of one great individual
creation. His imaginative insight into character in
general was no doubt considerable; his draughtsmanship,
whether as exhibited in the rough sketch or in the
finished portrait, is unquestionably most vigorous: but an
artist may put a hundred striking figures upon his canvas
for one that will linger in the memory of those who have
gazed upon it; and it is after all, I think, the one figure
of Captain Tobias Shandy which has graven itself in-
delibly on the memory of mankind. To have made this
single addition to the imperishable types of human character embodied in the world's literature may seem, as has
been said, but a light matter to those who talk with light
exaggeration of the achievements of the literary artist;
but if we exclude that one creative prodigy among men,
who has peopled a whole gallery with imaginary beings
more real than those of flesh and blood, we shall find that
very few archetypal creations have sprung from any
single hand. Now, My Uncle Toby is as much the
archetype of guileless good nature, of affectionate simplicity, as Hamlet is of irresolution, or Iago of cunning, or
Shylock of race-hatred; and he contrives to preserve all
the characteristics of an ideal type amid surroundings of
intensely prosaic realism, with which he himself, moreover, considered as an individual character in a specific

story, is in complete accord. If any one be disposed to underrate the creative and dramatic power to which this testifies, let him consider how it has commonly fared with those writers of prose fiction who have attempted to personify a virtue in a man. Take the work of another famous English humourist and sentimentalist, and compare Uncle Toby's manly and dignified gentleness of heart with the unreal " gush " of the Brothers Cheeryble, or the fatuous benevolence of Mr. Pickwick. We do not believe in the former, and we cannot but despise the latter. But Captain Shandy is reality itself, within and without; and though we smile at his naïveté, and may even laugh outright at his boyish enthusiasm for his military hobby, we never cease to respect him for a moment. There is no shirking or softening of the comic aspects of his character ; there could not be, of course, for Sterne needed him more, and used him more for his purposes as a humourist than for his purposes as a sentimentalist. Nay, it is on the rare occasions when he deliberately sentimentalizes with Captain Shandy, that the Captain is the least delightful ; it is then that the hand loses its cunning, and the stroke strays ; it is then, and only then, that the benevolence of the good soldier seems to verge, though ever so little, upon affectation. It is a pity, for instance, that Sterne should, in illustration of Captain Shandy's kindness of heart, have plagiarized (as he is said to have done) the incident of the torment-ing fly, caught and put out of the window with the words " Get thee gone, poor devil ! Why should I harm thee ? The world is surely large enough for thee and me." There is something too much of self-conscious virtue in the apostrophe. This we feel is not the real Uncle Toby of Sterne's objective mood ; it is the Uncle

Toby of the subjectifying sentimentalist, surveying his character through the false medium of his own hypertrophied sensibilities. These lapses, however, are fortunately rare. As a rule we see the worthy Captain only as he appeared to his creator's keen dramatic eye, and as he is set before us in a thousand exquisite touches of dialogue—the man of simple mind and soul, profoundly unimaginative and unphilosophical, but lacking not in a certain shrewd common-sense; exquisitely *naïf*, and delightfully *mal-à-propos* in his observations, but always pardonably, never foolishly, so; inexhaustibly amiable, but with no weak amiability; homely in his ways, but a perfect gentleman withal; in a word, the most winning and lovable personality that is to be met with, surely, in the whole range of fiction.

It is, in fact, with Sterne's general delineations of character as it is, I have attempted to show, with his particular passages of sentiment. He is never at his best and truest—as indeed no writer of fiction ever is or can be—save when he is allowing his dramatic imagination to play the most freely upon his characters, and thinking least about himself. This is curiously illustrated in his handling of what is perhaps the next most successful of the uncaricatured portraits in the Shandy gallery—the presentment of the Rev. Mr. Yorick. Nothing can be more perfect in its way than the picture of the "lively, witty, sensitive and heedless parson," in chapter x. of the first volume of *Tristram Shandy*. We seem to see the thin, melancholy figure on the rawboned horse—the apparition which could "never present itself in the village but it caught the attention of old and young," so that "labour stood still as he passed, the bucket hung suspended in the middle of the well, the spinning-wheel forgot its round;

even chuck-farthing and shuffle-cap themselves stood gaping till he was out of sight." Throughout this chapter Sterne, though describing himself, is projecting his personality to a distance as it were, and contemplating it dramatically; and the result is excellent. When in the next chapter he becomes "lyrical" so to speak; when the reflection upon his (largely imaginary) wrongs impels him to look inward, the invariable consequence follows : and though Yorick's much be-praised death-scene, with Eugenius at his bed-side, is redeemed from entire failure by an admixture of the humorous with its attempted pathos, we ask ourselves with some wonder what the unhappiness —or the death itself, for that matter—is "all about." The wrongs which were supposed to have broken Yorick's heart are most imperfectly specified (a comic proof, by the way, of Sterne's entire absorption in himself to the confusion of his own personal knowledge with that of the reader) and the first conditions of enlisting the reader's sympathies are left unfulfilled.

But it is comparatively seldom that this foible of Sterne obtrudes itself upon the strictly narrative and dramatic parts of his work ; and next to the abiding charm and interest of his principal figure, it is by the admirable life and colour of his scenes that he exercises his strongest powers of fascination over a reader. Perpetual as are Sterne's affectations, and tiresome as is his eternal self-consciousness when he is speaking in his own person, yet when once the dramatic instinct fairly lays hold of him there is no writer who ever makes us more completely forget him in the presence of his characters—none who can bring them and their surroundings, their looks and words, before us with such convincing force of reality. One wonders sometimes whether Sterne himself was

aware of the high dramatic excellence of many of what
actors would call his "carpenter's scenes"—the mere
interludes introduced to amuse us while the stage is being
prepared for one of those more elaborate and deliberate
displays of pathos or humour, which do not always turn
out to be unmixed successes when they come. Sterne
prided himself vastly upon the incident of Lefevre's death ;
but I dare say that there is many a modern reader who
would rather have lost this highly-wrought piece of
domestic drama, than that other exquisite little scene in
the kitchen of the inn, when Corporal Trim toasts the
bread which the sick lieutenant's son is preparing for his
father's posset, while "Mr. Yorick's curate was smoking
a pipe by the fire, but said not a word good or bad to
comfort the youth." The whole scene is absolute life ;
and the dialogue between the corporal and the parson,
as related by the former to his master, with Captain
Shandy's comments thereon, is almost Shakespearean in
its excellence. Says the corporal :—

When the lieutenant had taken his glass of sack and toast
he felt himself a little revived, and sent down into the kitchen
to let me know that in about ten minutes he should be glad if
I would step upstairs. I believe, said the landlord, he is going
to say his prayers, for there was a book laid on the chair by the
bed-side, and as I shut the door I saw him take up a cushion.
I thought, said the curate, that you gentlemen of the army, Mr.
Trim, never said your prayers at all. I heard the poor gentleman say his prayers last night, said the landlady, very devoutly
and with my own ears, or I could not have believed it. Are you
sure of it ? replied the curate. A soldier, an' please your reverence, said I, prays as often (of his own accord) as a parson ; and
when he is fighting for his king, and for his own life, and for
his honour too, he has the most reason to pray to God of any
one in the whole world. 'Twas well said of thee, Trim, said my

uncle Toby. But when a soldier, said I, an' please your reverence, has been standing for twelve hours together in the
trenches, up to his knees in cold water—or engaged, said I, for
months together in long and dangerous marches; harassed,
perhaps, in his rear to-day; harassing others to-morrow; de-
tached here; countermanded there; resting this night out
upon his arms; beat up in his shirt the next; benumbed in his
joints; perhaps without straw in his tent to kneel on, [he] must
say his prayers how and when he can. I believe, said I—for I
was piqued, quoth the corporal, for the reputation of the army—
I believe, an't please your reverence, said I, that when a
soldier gets time to pray, he prays as heartily as a parson—
though not with all his fuss and hypocrisy. Thou shouldst
not have said that, Trim, said my uncle Toby; for God only
knows who is a hypocrite, and who is not. At the great and
general review of us all, corporal, at the day of judgment (and
not till then) it will be seen who have done their duties in this
world, and who have not, and we shall be advanced, Trim, accordingly. I hope we shall, said Trim. It is in the Scripture, said
my uncle Toby, and I will show it thee in the morning. In the
meantime, we may depend upon it, Trim, for our comfort, said
my uncle Toby; that God Almighty is so good and just a
governor of the world, that if we have but done our duties in
it, it will never be inquired into whether we have done them in
a red coat or a black one. I hope not, said the corporal. But
go on, said my uncle Toby, with thy story.

We might almost fancy ourselves listening to that noble
prose colloquy between the disguised king and his soldiers
on the night before Agincourt, in *Henry V*. And though
Sterne does not, of course, often reach this level of
dramatic dignity, there are passages in abundance in
which his dialogue assumes, through sheer force of indi-
vidualized character, if not all the dignity, at any rate all
the impressive force and simplicity of the "grand style."

Taken altogether, however, his place in English letters

is hard to fix, and his tenure in. human memory hard to
determine. Hitherto he has held his own, with the great
writers of his era, but it has been in virtue, as I have
attempted to show, of a contribution to the literary
possessions of mankind which is as uniquely limited in
amount as it is exceptionally perfect in quality. One
cannot but feel that, as regards the sum of his titles to
recollection, his name stands far below either of those
other two which in the course of the last century added
themselves to the highest rank among the classics of
English humour. Sterne has not the abounding life and
the varied human interest of Fielding : and to say nothing
of his vast intellectual inferiority to Swift, he never so
much as approaches those problems of everlasting con-
cernment to man which Swift handles with so terrible a
fascination. Certainly no enthusiastic Gibbon of the
future is ever likely to say of Sterne's " pictures of human
manners," that they will " outlive the palace of the Es-
curial and the Imperial Eagle of the House of Austria."
Assuredly no one will ever find in *this* so-called English
antitype of the Curé of Meudon, any of the deeper
qualities of that gloomy and commanding spirit which
has been finely compared to the " soul of Rabelais
habitans in sicco." Nay, to descend even to minor apti-
tudes, Sterne cannot tell a story as Swift and Fielding
can tell one : and his work is not assured of life as *Tom
Jones* and *Gulliver's Travels*, considered as stories alone,
would be assured of it—even if the one were stripped of
its cheerful humour, and the other disarmed of its savage
allegory. And hence it might be rash to predict that
Sterne's days will be as long in the land of literary
memory as the two great writers aforesaid. Ranked, as
he still is, among " English classics," he undergoes, I

suspect, even more than an English classic's ordinary share of reverential neglect. Among those who talk about him, he has, I should imagine, fewer readers than Fielding, and very much fewer than Swift. Nor is he likely to increase their number as time goes on, but rather perhaps the contrary. Indeed the only question is whether with the lapse of years he will not, like other writers as famous in their day, become yet more of a mere name. For there is still, of course, a further stage to which he may decline. That object of so much empty mouth-honour, the English classic of the last and earlier centuries, presents himself for classification under three distinct categories. There is the class who are still read in a certain measure, though in a much smaller measure than is pretended, by the great body of ordinarily well-educated men. Of this class, the two authors whose names I have already cited, Swift and Fielding, are typical examples ; and it may be taken to include Gold-smith also. Then comes the class of those whom the ordinarily well-educated public, whatever they may pre-tend, read really very little or not at all : and in this class we may couple Sterne with Addison, with Smollett, and, except of course as to Robinson Crusoe—unless, indeed, our *blasé* boys have outgrown him among other pleasures of boyhood—with Defoe. But below this there is yet a third class of writers, who are not only read by none but the critic, the connoisseur, or the historian of literature, but are scarcely read even by them, except from curiosity, or " in the way of business." The type of this class is Richardson : and one cannot, I say, help asking whether he will hereafter have Sterne as a compa-nion of his dusty solitude. Are *Tristram Shandy* and the *Sentimental Journey* destined to descend from the second

class into the third—from the region of partial into that
of total neglect, and to have their portion with *Clarissa
Harlowe* and *Sir Charles Grandison*? The unbounded
vogue which they enjoyed in their time will not save
them : for sane and sober critics compared Richardson in
his day to Shakespeare, and Diderot broke forth into
prophetic rhapsodies upon the immortality of his works
which to us in these days have become absolutely
pathetic in their felicity of falsified prediction. Seeing,
too, that a good three-fourths of the attractions which
won Sterne his contemporary popularity are now so much
dead weight of dead matter, and that the vital residuum
is in amount so small, the fate of Richardson might seem
to be but too close behind him. Yet it is difficult to
believe that this fate will ever quite overtake him. His
sentiment may have mostly ceased—it probably has
ceased, to stir any emotion at all in these days ; but there
is an imperishable element in his humour. And though
the circle of his readers may have no tendency to increase,
one can hardly suppose that a charm, which those who
still feel it feel so keenly, will ever entirely cease to
captivate ; or that time can have any power over a perfume
which so wonderfully retains the pungent freshness of its
fragrance after the lapse of a hundred years.

THE END.

PRINTED BY GILBERT AND RIVINGTON, LIMITED, ST. JOHN'S SQUARE, LONDON.

For EU product safety concerns, contact us at Calle de José Abascal, 56–1°,
28003 Madrid, Spain or eugpsr@cambridge.org.